High praise for
WOMENTALITY
edited by Erin Wildermuth

WILDERMUTH, A FREELANCE writer and travel enthusiast, offers up a stellar collection of stories from women around the globe who bucked nine-to-five jobs to go into business for themselves. . . . This inspiring collection makes a strong case for how women can design their work lives to meet both personal and professional needs.
  PUBLISHERS WEEKLY, starred review

GET OUT YOUR pen and paper and prepare to take notes on Erin Wildermuth's short volume *Womentality*, a collection of stories from thirteen women who abandoned the traditional workplace and reclaimed the reins to their lives.
  FOREWORD REVIEWS, Lit Hit: Indie Books That Will Blow You Away!

IN THE FUTURE, people will be able to work from any location, at any time, and live life completely on their own terms. What if the future is now? Wildermuth lets thirteen women who found success as freelancers tell their encouraging stories here. . . . Striking out on your own can seem imposing, but women seeking a professional change may find a biography that resonates in this book.
  BOOKLIST

IN *WOMENTALITY*, EDITOR Erin Wildermuth calls attention to a burgeoning trend for workplace independence with essays from thirteen women who've all said, "Enough is enough!" to their jobs. These are not professional writers—they are nurses, accountants, teachers and IT specialists who speak plain and write with passion, whether they've given up a long commute or are fleeing from a failing economy. The book progresses from accounts of the initial "aha" moment to step-by-step advice on how to forge self-employment without much more than pluck and a strong internet connection. Their courage is inspiring.
  KAREN HILDEBRAND, author and poet, *Crossing Pleasure Avenue;*
  former HR manager

WOMEN ARE OFTEN expected to sacrifice for and adapt to a world that seems designed around the needs of someone else. In *Womentality*, Erin Wildermuth has collected essays that show how the sometimes-maligned "gig economy" has empowered women, giving them choice and control through self-employment. The essays demonstrate that this is not an option only for women in rich Western countries, but a universal opportunity. Breaking away from the traditional role of an employee is instrumental even—maybe especially—in countries where women fight discrimination and poverty.

    JANET BUFTON, co-founder and program coordinator, Institute for Liberal Studies, Ottawa, Canada

WOMENTALITY'S TOPIC IS so important. It is eye-opening and empowering to read about these women harnessing technology to take charge of their careers and their lives. They show us possibilities for women around the world and for ourselves.

    JESSICA BACAL, M.F.A., ED.D., director, Smith College Narratives Project; editor, *Mistakes I Made at Work*

THESE ESSAYS ARE particularly relevant in the #MeToo era, where women are more empowered than ever to stand up for themselves. Even though each essay recounts a unique story from women across the globe, I found myself strongly identifying with the frustrations and setbacks they faced in the workplace. This collection left me inspired by their courage and full of ideas on how to reclaim power in my own professional life.

    LISA GAILLOUD, community organizer

WOMENTALITY

WOMENTALITY

THIRTEEN **EMPOWERING** STORIES
BY EVERYDAY **WOMEN** WHO SAID
GOODBYE TO THE **WORKPLACE**
AND **HELLO** TO THEIR **LIVES**

Edited by
ERIN WILDERMUTH

THREE ROOMS PRESS
New York, NY

WOMENTALITY: Thirteen Empowering Stories by Everyday Women Who Said Goodbye to the Workplace and Hello to Their Lives
EDITED BY Erin Wildermuth

© 2019 by Three Rooms Press

ISBN 978-1-941110-84-3 (trade paperback original)
ISBN 978-1-941110-85-0 (Ebook)
Library of Congress Control Number: 2019938491

TRP-079

Publication Date: October 8, 2019

BISAC category code
BUS025000: Business & Economics/Entrepreneurship
BUS109000: Business & Economics/Women in Business
SEL027000: Self-Help/Personal Growth/Success

COVER AND BOOK DESIGN:
KG Design International: www.katgeorges.com

DISTRIBUTED BY:
PGW/Ingram: www.pgw.com

Three Rooms Press
New York, NY
www.threeroomspress.com
info@threeroomspress.com

TABLE OF CONTENTS

FOREWORD

LEAVING THE WORKFORCE HAS BECOME A cultural obsession in the United States. Perhaps it started in 2007 with the bestselling book *The 4-Hour Workweek*, but probably not. Timothy Ferriss's *New York Times* bestseller was an indication of a trend that had been brewing for some time. His story is also far from the norm. A CEO who was already raking in $40,000 a month, Tim focused on automatizing his already successful business. His first few chapters concentrate on building the right kind of business for working the least number of hours. He spends his days learning languages and dancing the tango. Economies would not function if everyone followed his example, though the world might be filled with better dancers.

Does this mean we're all destined for long hours, exhaustion, and economic abuse? Not necessarily. Work doesn't have to be a grind. It doesn't have to be demeaning. Though working only four hours a week *en masse* might not sustain our collective livelihoods right now, we can all work significantly fewer than forty hours. We can work at varied paces and in variable hours. We can fashion our work to align with our own values and chosen lifestyles. Contrary to what many of us have been sold, work can be an inspired process that evolves with us throughout our lives.

This is the life of the self-employed. Today, most societies still focus on full-time, 9-to-5, employer-driven work. But more and more people (millions of them[1]) are finding ways to define their own work/life balance through creativity and innovation. This book is about some of them—all women—their journeys, their struggles, and their quests for happiness in their careers and day-to-day life.

This is not a book about people who drive fancy cars, frequent swanky nightclubs, or measure their worth in extravagance. It isn't about exploiting currency differences, making smart investments, or outsourcing labor to amass wealth.

Most of all, this is not a book about people who do not work. It is a book about people who work hard to maintain a livelihood outside of rigid employee-employer relationships. It is a book about women triumphing over a system that traditionally pays them far less than men. Instead of selling forty hours of their time each week, they choose how they

---

1 "10 Facts About American Workers" https://pewrsr.ch/2YL6C9d

work, when they work, and why they work. With every contract, they choose anew.

These stories have been sourced internationally to illustrate that a life of workplace independence does not need to be reserved for a wealthy elite. In fact, people whose local economies have failed them may have the most to gain. Though the challenges of working for oneself differ from country to country, our increasingly connected world makes this type of work possible for everyone. As the contributors in this book will attest: it isn't easy, but it's worth it.

—ERIN WILDERMUTH, *May 2019*

WOMENTALITY

Name: Lauren Gerber

Nationality: South African

Country of Residence: South Africa

Why She Left the Rat Race: When given the opportunity to work from home one day a week, Lauren found that the freedom to work on her own terms invigorated every aspect of her life. Not only was she more productive at work, but she was able to accomplish other goals. This propelled her towards freelancing full-time.

CHAPTER ONE
The Great Escape: My Path Out of the Rat Race
by Lauren Gerber, *South Africa*

ONE MOMENT, ONE CONVERSATION, ONE EVENT can change your life forever. Short or long, profound or simple, it can instantly impact every level of your being. I know this, because it happened to me. During an ordinary day, during an ordinary moment, an ordinary conversation set me on an extraordinary path that would eventually put me in control of my life for the first time.

Picture a bus stop in a nondescript town. Picture a girl standing there, waiting. That girl is me. Three years ago, I still didn't know what I wanted to do with my career or my life. I was caught up in a web of work that didn't lead anywhere. Having worked for multiple companies, I knew it all felt the same. I started each new job hoping that I would feel differently or that something would change. Nothing did. Staring into space, I hoped I could get home quickly. I felt tired. The bus came and I paid my fees and took a seat on a two-seater bench, alone. There weren't many people. I was finally heading home.

As I gazed out the window, distracted, a conversation broke into my wandering thoughts. An ordinary looking, middle-aged man, sat directly opposite me. If I had to put money on it, I would say he had kids and a wife. He told the person next to him that he was really sick. He had just been to work, to get permission from his boss to visit the doctor. He was on his way there, to the doctor, now. Upon his return, he would be required to produce a note for his employer.

An ordinary conversation, an ordinary event. I imagine most people wouldn't have given it a second thought. Perhaps, on a different day, I wouldn't have either. This day was different. I never stopped thinking about this man and what I heard. The memory, three years later, still pierces through me. Alarm bells went off in my head. I felt deeply sorry for this man. He was older. He was weathered. He clearly had vast amounts of life experience. He had a family and children that he cared for deeply. He was feeling really ill and was concerned about his health, and he had to get permission to see a health professional.

To me, this was anything but normal.

I questioned his situation on every level. Why did this man have to ask his boss permission to go and see his own doctor? Why did someone else have a say over decisions regarding his health? Why did he have to stay at work until the time of his appointment? He was an adult. He was independently running a home, looking after children, supporting a wife and maintaining a job. Surely this individual should not have had to ask permission to see a doctor? A boss is not a medical professional, they are the leader of a company. There is a fundamental difference. Moreover, he was asked to return with proof of his visit? Why does a grown man need to prove he was at the doctor? What was wrong with this picture?

My life experiences, lessons, and teachings would not amount to me being treated like a child in a company environment. I did not want to be at the mercy of a boss or manager granting me permission to see a doctor. In fact, I did not want to be at the mercy of a boss or manager to micromanage any aspect of my life.

It was more than sad. It was unjust, a sign of a much deeper societal problem. At that moment I promised myself that I would not end up like this man. My life experiences, lessons, and teachings would not amount to me being treated like a child in a company environment. I did not want to be at the mercy of a boss or manager granting me permission to see a doctor. In fact, I did not want to be at the mercy of a boss or manager to micromanage any aspect of my life.

I needed things to change. Otherwise I would end up just like the man on the bus, and the many people like him. That thought terrified me to the ends of the earth and back.

I started out in the world enthusiastic, hopeful, and excited about the possibilities of work. Having studied psychology and criminology, I spent years working all sorts of jobs. I moved from company to company, building a skill set in digital marketing and copywriting. Everything fell into place for me in the corporate world. I had always loved writing. I loved research and technology. It all seemed to make sense and getting jobs became easier and easier.

> **Unexpected Lifestyle Changes:**
>
> Lauren's relationship with money changed when she started to earn as an entrepreneur instead of as an employee. She spent less, but it felt freeing. She found that she needed fewer things as she gained more of her life back.

But at some point, I began to notice trends that didn't sit well with my vision of what a just world should resemble. Employees were weighted down with too many requirements. They had set hours, permissions, roles, and responsibilities. They often helped build a company from the ground up. They invested time, effort, and huge chunks of their lives into these companies. People were often loyal and felt beholden to their companies. But companies, I noticed, did not reciprocate.

It wasn't a two-way street.

Companies employed people until technology advanced and their needs shifted. Then, those employees became disposable. This became a pattern in my life. Repeatedly, I was hired until I was made redundant, companies closed down, or they found someone to work longer hours for less money. Every time this happened, I fell back into a new round of employment. I went through this for a good couple of years.

Throughout these cycles of starting new jobs, I learned more about myself than I did anything else. There was one job in particular which really laid the groundwork for my escape from the rat race. Others tolerated it, but for me, it was the final straw.

At this job, everyone at the top acted unprofessionally. The environment was sleazy—salaries were

increased due to personal relationships and favor-
itism. Management was fickle and unpredictable,
and the staff constantly worried about job security.
People stabbed each other in the back in a desperate attempt to stay afloat and to make sure their
jobs were secure. It was an impossible environment,
but we all needed our salaries. I tried to be as
authentic as I could by always standing up for what I
believed was right. It was important to me that I
lived my life according to my own morals, that I
stayed true to myself.

Throughout my time at this company, I resolved
to never choose a salary over my dignity. I stood up
for people and became the office advocate, the
person who deeply cared about everyone and tried
to protect them. Eventually, the company ran into
financial problems and one Christmas we didn't get
paid. In fact, we didn't get paid throughout the
entire Christmas holiday, New Year's, or the beginning of the next year. We were finally paid in the
middle of January.

This deeply impacted me. My financial resources
were not designed to take a prolonged period of
unexplained and unexcused paycheck delays, but I
was one of the lucky ones. The people at the bottom
of the heap were living paycheck-to-paycheck. They
truly suffered. The cleaning staff could not buy

their children Christmas presents. You can imagine how their families were impacted as this pay freeze continued beyond the holiday season.

I was done. I vowed never to work in an office again, but I had no idea how I was going to pull this off.

I live in South Africa, where the infrastructure leaves much to be desired. We trail behind first-world countries in many ways. Unfortunately, this is a huge obstacle to escaping an office environment. I could not live for months on end without a salary. I needed cash quickly. I was in no position to play around with time.

> **The Best Thing About Work Beyond Wages:**
> "I never dread Monday. I never wait for Friday. I am relaxed and content every single day of the week. I never wish pieces of my life away."

The decision to flee is easy once you become aware of the challenges. This is the stage where most people give up. It takes a certain level of commitment to look at your bank balance turning red, to hear all your loved ones telling you to return to the corporate world, and to still decide to fight harder rather than give up. I was sick to death of the 9-to-5 rubbish, the clock watching, and the time that was being taken from my life.

I had already had a taste of self-employment

and knew what my life could look like. It was this small taste of freedom that kept my commitment rock solid.

> **Top Tips:**
>
> "Live your life according to your own ideals and expectations. Find the lifestyle that allows you to appreciate every day, and then live that life."

One of my previous employers had a policy allowing us to work from home one day each week. I found that on that day, I woke up happier. I felt calm and relaxed. I wasn't watching the clock or desperately awaiting the weekend. I had more energy to go to the gym on those days and I felt better in general. Every week, month after month, that one day felt different.

This made me absolutely certain that working at home would be the ideal situation for me. It would get me away from office politics and it would save me from the trivial talk and unproductive, destructive gossip.

I signed up on a few freelance websites and within a few weeks, I had landed my first clients. I started writing books, sales copy, and much more. I enjoyed it, but it was incredibly stressful not knowing how much money I would have at the end of each month.

Despite my resolve, I kept my eye on job portals, eyeing full-time positions. I passed up some amazing opportunities. That's how I knew I could make it. I could make it because I had to. No matter what the salary on offer, no matter how much I was struggling on my own, I was determined to never go back to an office environment. The challenge was real. The bills were real. The pressure from family and friends was real. Fortunately, around that time I found the perfect segue job. It was a corporate job for a big company, but entirely remote. After a series of interviews, I got the job. I worked there for two years.

It was a great experience. The salary was not what I could have gotten, but I was thrilled to have a stable job on my own terms. It was a winning combination for me. Not only did the job allow me to work from home, but it also had flexible hours. During these two years, I found myself working weekends and holidays. I never recorded overtime or asked for extra pay. I was working because I wanted to, because I saw my own work as a product of my efforts and I wanted it to be awesome. I couldn't believe how much better focused I was and how productive I could be when I was treated like an adult.

Perhaps the best part of the job was that I finally had enough time to work on myself. I was able to commit to going to the gym and to eating consciously. I worked on all aspects of myself mentally, spiritually, and socially. I had a great balance between work, life, friends, and everything else—I could even go to doctor's appointments on my own schedule. I loved every second of my life.

When this opportunity ended after two years, I knew I had found happiness and I wasn't about to let it go. Once you've tasted how sweet life can be when you truly own yourself and your time it's impossible to go back. I spent a good couple of months signing up for every flexi-job, remote opportunity, and freelance gig available.

My transition out of the rat race took time, ingenuity, and some major lifestyle changes.

Early on, I spent nearly all my free time working. I spent nights working. I spent early mornings working. I gave up all my weekends. But working wasn't the hardest part. Finding clients and negotiating prices was tricky. If you aren't careful, it is easy to find yourself in a race to the bottom in terms in terms of pay and even how you are treated by clients. New clients don't trust you at first, some jobs aren't well suited to you, and many clients want the best possible deal for the least amount of money. Finding the right balance was difficult. Sometimes, I had to work for very low amounts, because at the end of each month I needed to have some money to pay my bills. Especially in the beginning, you need to take what you can get. When you are working for yourself, nothing is guaranteed. Learning my own value while building a client base who trusted that value was not an overnight affair. This is where ingenuity came into play.

Early on I spent nearly all my free time working. I spent nights working. I spent early mornings working. I gave up all my weekends. But working wasn't the hardest part. Finding clients and negotiating prices was tricky. If you aren't careful, it is easy to find yourself in a race to the bottom

---

I became obsessed with business shows and dedicated to learning from people who made their own money. I did my best to speak to business owners, freelancers, and other professionals who worked for themselves. I decided to diversify. I took measures to make myself more attractive to an international clientele and began to develop relationships with clients throughout the world.

My relationship with money also started to change. I felt the worth of every penny I earned. I realized how hard people work for money. I thought about this each time I was tempted to buy something I didn't need. Before working for myself, I was the girl that would enjoy buying loads of extras without thinking much about where the money came from, or what I had to do to earn it. I no longer thought this way, but it didn't feel restraining. Instead, it felt wonderful. My bills were no longer marked with red numbers. All the numbers were black.

I had successfully escaped from the 9-to-5 rat race.

I wasn't an overnight success. I gave up a lot by leaving the 9-to-5 lifestyle. I cried tears of pure frustration many times over. I lost many nights of sleep. There were times I wanted to give up.

I am so glad I didn't. What I have gained is priceless. I never dread Monday. I never wait for Friday. I am relaxed and content every single day of the week. I never wish pieces of my life away. Freedom means different things to different people. For me, freedom is about being an independent adult who is able to make my own decisions. I am in control of my body and my time. I can work as little or as much as I want. At the end of the day, the consequences or rewards are mine alone.

I am proud that I was able to rise above and find work with little more than an internet connection. I can happily say that I did it and I am still doing it. It has now been nearly three full years since I have worked in an office—nearly three full years since I overheard that conversation on the bus—and I couldn't be prouder. I have room to breathe and be myself. I can work in my own space. No one is looking over my shoulder or micromanaging my hours. All my moments are mine, and I wouldn't wish them away for the world.

I look outside my window every day at the congestion and traffic and I am thankful that I am not a part of it. I am now in a good place. I am happy to report that I have reached not only my career goals but also my personal ones. I don't regret the choices I have made and the path that I have chosen. If I had to give advice to anybody out there I would tell them that you don't need to live your life according to everyone else's ideals and expectations. Rather, live your life according to your own. I march to my own beat and I am, after many years, 100 percent happy with that.

The possibilities for my future are endless. Every single one is completely mine to pursue.

Name: Emily Schwartz

Nationality: American

Country of Residence: United States

Why She Left the Rat Race: Emily grew up in wide open spaces, full of drive and creativity. The transition from college to the American workforce killed those attributes. She was willing to do whatever it took to get them back, and eventually realized that taking full control of her own life was the only way to live.

CHAPTER TWO
The Fear and The Farm
Emily Schwartz, *United States*

I WAS FALLING IN LOVE WHEN all my buried insecurities began to pour out of me. They started like water from a leaky faucet, slow occasional drops that didn't cause notice or make more than a hollow ping. As I found my life tangling up with someone else's, the pings and pangs began to sound more frequently. They rang louder each time. The drops began to form a steady stream. Then the pipe blew and water rushed out with alarming strength, force, and destructive power.

I've read articles about how a partner can act as a mirror, but it's not a magic mirror. It doesn't show you what you want to see, it shows you what you need to see. The view can be brutal. It was for me.

Before I met Bryan, I was busy discovering myself. I had graduated in 2009, with the recession in full swing. My self-employed, carpenter father hadn't gotten a call for employment in over six months. We survived on my mom's paychecks and the inheritance of my great aunt who had recently passed away. I looked at colleges, but I didn't see much point in accumulating debt when it was very likely I wouldn't get a job when I graduated. My dad told me the economy would bounce back. He tried to encourage me by accompanying me on visits to college campuses. In the end, I decided to go to community college and felt excited to do so.

The next six years were a whirlwind. I spent my time going to classes and working, making new connections, and maintaining old friendships. Young adulthood is all about creating memories, and season after season I built mine. Getting too drunk at bars and having long conversations on the patio as we burned through packs of cigarettes were as much a part of my education as my classes. Friends and I explored longing and heightened emotions as we gazed at our infatuations—people we wanted to explore with our lips and fingertips.

I was on top of the world, living life to the fullest as I discovered myself. I opened up to others and they opened up to me. I fell in love with my classes, where I led discussions whenever I could. I overcame my shortcomings in math. I learned archery. I took a dream study course. I lost 25 pounds and ran miles in wooded parks. I worked with a horse trainer as a catch rider, showing other people's horses, and even trained a young gelding from start to finish. I took my dog, Tess, to obedience and agility classes, and then I started taking her everywhere. I moved out to the west side of Cleveland and came back to the farm on weekends just to visit her. I became *me*, the one you find after the mold of high school is shattered, and you're left with a fresh ball of clay you can sculpt over the next decade.

My life was a raw experience in the rust belt during the post-recession that was uniquely my own. It inspired an equally beautiful future. I had plans. I was going to create my own graphic novel and be this badass self-employed writer, artist, and designer.

Even my base was beautiful. My life was a raw experience in the rust belt during the post-recession that was uniquely my own. It inspired an equally beautiful future. I had plans. I was going to create my own graphic novel and be this badass self-employed writer, artist, and designer.

I didn't feel the tiniest drop of insecurity.

Bryan and I met on a chilly spring night in early April. I was only a month from graduating with my associate degree and the wind carried the sweet scent of warming weather. In anticipation of the change of season, I traded a stuffy night on the couch for an evening adventure out on the town.

Unexpected Lifestyle Changes: Turning towards entrepreneurship helped Emily to overcome self-doubt. She gained confidence in her abilities and began to trust herself.

Love at first sight is a corny cliché, but I understand the turn of phrase. It's not falling *in love* at first sight. It's that soft inward smile, the spike of your heart, and the intuitive voice that says, "Ah, there you are. I've been waiting for you."

I found myself amazed by this man. His adventures through the Southwest and mysterious deserts kept us talking all night. Bryan had taken his small student loan and driven his car until it broke down in New Mexico. He settled for a bit, working and making friends. Then he traveled to the coast, moving in and out of scrappy apartments with punks and outcasts. He had been living life far from where he had grown up, out of his comfort zone, but happy with the adventure of his new beginnings.

This story wasn't unfamiliar to me. Three of my four older sisters had done similar things. They had traveled far from home—to college, to move across the country, or to explore Europe. I had grown up hearing these stories and they always fascinated me, and yet gave me the slightest twinge of jealousy and self-doubt. Bryan rekindled these feelings, sparking them into a new flame in my heart—and a desire for more.

My memories weren't like his. I had gone to a rural high school where things came easily. He spent his youth running through city streets at night with his heart pounding in his ears. He made a point to do things he had never done before, just to feel the thrill.

My memories were safer, they were soft.

Growing up as an artistic kid on a horse farm in the Midwest, I would often get home from school, tack up my horse, and gallop across hay fields in the warmth of the setting sun. I loved the thrill of climbing up in the saddle, the earthy scent of horse and rich leather in my nose. My adventures were in nature, and sometimes in my imagination. We would canter off into the fields to slay dragons or fight off the monsters in the woods.

Warm spring nights were spent sleeping on hay bales in the barn as my sisters and I eagerly awaited for the broodmares to give birth to their foals. The excitement would be tangible as the lady of the hour began to circle her stall. We could taste the salty scent of her sweat hitting the damp cool air. Within minutes a beautiful, perfect tiny horse laid at her side shivering and looking at the new world with bright, liquid eyes.

Summers were for working with the calves, pigs, and horses in preparation for the county fair in September. My sisters and I would proudly present our beloved animals to friends, family, the local community, and the fair judges. We often took home ribbons, though the lessons and the memories have proven more durable.

Fall days weren't spent playing in leaves like suburban kids. We woke up early to load up the trailer, groom the horses, and set off to the local parks. Endless miles were eaten away under quick hooves. My definition of feeling alive was made under these crisp, blue October skies.

Winter nights weren't always indoors cuddled up next to the fireplace. When the moon was full and the snow was thick, the hayfields transformed into a landscape from a faraway planet. The woods silently watched as my dogs and I ran as fast as we could through the night, cold air burning my lungs. My need to run further and faster only made them burn more.

Art and literature were as familiar as the farm. I devoured fiction and wrote endlessly. My writing and art often mingled into child-created masterpieces: picture books with elaborate stories and strange characters that were half-human, half-beast.

My first eighteen years were magical in their own right, but when I compared them to the traveling, urban adventures that Bryan recounted, they somehow fell short. Jealousy rang strongly in my ears. I looked back and felt like someone who missed out on teenage years. Instead of being proud of my wholesome, rich upbringing, I felt naive. Bryan never said anything to make me feel that way. He thought my memories were as interesting as I found his. He smiled as I recalled autumn days spent riding, summers working with animals, delivering baby horses in the spring, and winter nights in the field. I wish I could have seen myself through his eyes, instead of feeling embarrassed by all the things I felt I had missed. The insecurities must have been there all along, but the mirror of my relationship brought them sharply into focus.

> **The Best Thing About Work Beyond Wages:**
> The passion that had faded in the workforce returned in full swing. Emily has been able to spend quality time with her family, horse, and dogs. She has returned to her art and writing. She's taken up cooking. "The best part," she writes, "is I now know I can."

After graduation, I found a customer service job at an equine supply facility. Soon, I was promoted to the design team. It was a small business, and I began to learn how the trade worked. I hadn't reached my dream goals yet, but I was intent on exceeding expectations.

A few months later discussions about the past started making me anxious and jealous. I found the pings and pangs coming more frequently. I found myself getting angry when Bryan talked about his adventures. I found myself comparing every detail and starting to idealize his past. He was six years my senior and I started feeling like his kid sister. My fears and insecurities, slowly but surely, began to drive me into a world of anxiety and depression.

Over the next year I learned what office life was about. My eager gaze, once hungry for absorbing new things, had dulled in the mundane, repetitive office atmosphere. I had gained weight. I found myself often irritated with Bryan and couldn't control my bouts of anxiety, anger, depression, and jealousy. I started hating everything about my life.

One night in the darkness of a long winter a particularly persistent whisper of doubt got the best of me. I had told Bryan a few times that one day I would like to move. This was a sore spot between us, because he had a new job that was just what he wanted, and where he wanted to stay for a long time. My gut twisted at staying somewhere and settling, and it hurt when I considered the idea of never moving out of state.

I cried that I couldn't stay. Never have I felt such pain. Never have I seen such pain in someone else. Bryan understood. He wanted me to experience that part of life. But he was in a different stage. His wanderlust was gone. He was ready to settle down, to make enough money that we could travel a bit and enjoy life with our dogs. He was ready for simpler things, but a small voice told me I was not. Neither of us could imagine a life without

Top Tip:
"Take the road less traveled."

the other, but neither could bear the pain of holding the other back from being happy.

Without the strong foundation of our relationship, I think we would have fallen apart. I wrestled with myself. It wasn't really the wanderlust that gnawed at me, it was the loss of purpose I felt in my life. I didn't understand why or how to fix it. It's what we all desire, isn't it? The feeling of purpose, that deep-rooted knowledge that we are giving a piece of ourselves to this world before we leave. I had felt it so strongly in my childhood and early adulthood. Yet now the flames had gone out. I was left with a hollow shell of a human, not the full-bodied adventurer I once envisioned. I despised what I thought I had become.

In that moment I realized that my inability to find happiness within myself could cost me the love of my life.

The cliché of self-discovery is to go hunting for purpose and self on a long-winded travel expedition, but that doesn't mean it is the only way. It may not even be the best way. How many people come home from their travels only to find themselves still not living the lives they want? I needed to rekindle my own creativity. I needed those days spent in the saddle, those all-day rides that had somehow become obsolete with age, so I could truly feel alive again. I didn't need to move somewhere far away and experience life elsewhere, I needed to love and accept myself to be happy no matter where I was.

With time and consideration, my urge to travel was replaced by newfound clarity and focus. My wanderlust had grown in reaction to my unhappiness. The unhappiness itself had taken seed from learning what was expected of me as an adult. I had become an office worker. It was terrible. Over the next couple of months, I came to terms with the fact that my work was draining the happiness from me. I drove two hours every day to a place that brought me no creative drive or passion. I needed those things back. I wanted to control how I lived and what I did. I did not want to let a company dictate my every move simply because they had steady pay and benefits.

What had happened to my dream of becoming a self-employed writer, artist, and designer? I needed a challenge and I needed to prove to myself that I could do this.

I began researching the logistics of working for myself. I picked up some marketing skills at work and spoke with my sister who had worked as a freelancer for years in the design field. I had apprenticed with her in California before graduation and it had left an impression. It was a brief taste of the life I could have, a life that was fully my own.

I found myself learning new things every day. I created a new image of myself that I could sell to clients in order to eventually pay the bills. I balanced my office job as I nurtured and grew this seed. I was completely engulfed in my new work and what it entailed. I realized I had found exactly what I wanted to do. Even better, it would allow me to live the life I so badly yearned for—the life I needed.

It took time, and I still wrestle with the small voice in my head that whispers without reason, but I began to heal.

I overcame my self-doubt. I began to focus and found that I could accomplish whatever I put my mind to. I reveled in this reality. I finally let go of the past and the baby sister image that had been haunting me. My jealousy towards Bryan faded as I realized that my story, my experiences were equal, unique, and all my own. I began to love everything about my new life, even the ups and downs that working for yourself entails. The whole journey was a thrill, and I found myself pouring every ounce of energy into each new project I took on.

Every step of the way, Bryan offered his absolute support. There was never a moment of doubt, not a word of negativity. Only the encouragement, the needed hugs, and wiping away of tears when I felt myself waver. On October 27th, 2017, I finally said goodbye for good to my office job. I would miss my work family, but it was time to take the final step. I couldn't have asked for a better send off.

It was a warm fall day. The sun shone against a deep blue sky, a sky filled with fluffy, white clouds that rolled lazily across the huge expanse. Wind rustled the fiery colored leaves that filled the tree-tops as I stood outside the building, looking nowhere in particular. I realized that this was it. This was where my path split, and I had decided to take the road less traveled.

The decision has been life-changing. I've been able to take my niece and nephew on a trip to Washington DC. I've become a passionate cook. I've returned to my art and writing. The clients I have met across the world have reignited my passion for riding my horse and working with my dogs. This spring I begin training for a 25-mile competitive trail ride that will take place in the fall. I am taking our youngest dog to agility classes. The best part is I now know I can.

Every evening, Bryan gets home from work and I wrap my arms around him with that same "I've been waiting for you" feeling. Since becoming this new, more secure version of myself, we have only become a stronger, more loving and compassionate team. It's not to say I still don't have my moments of doubt and insecurities, but they are far and few between.

We have a lot more experiences and adventures to come. We've only just started this new life together. But I've never felt so sure of anything in my entire life, I know we can do this, I know *I* can do this. At the end of every day I am thankful for my passion to pursue this dream, the loving support of my best friend, and the life I have chosen to live.

Name: Yanique P. Walters-Dynott

Nationality: Jamaican

Country of Residence: Jamaica

Why She Left the Rat Race: Yanique grew up watching her role models "hustle" to put food on the table. As the first college graduate in her family, she had access to the traditional workforce in Jamaica, but it wasn't what she chose. Instead, her education made her realize that "hustling can be called something else: entrepreneurship."

CHAPTER THREE
Finding and Sharing Freelancing
Yanique P. Walters-Dynott, *Jamaica*

GROWING UP I VOWED TO BE the one to take my mother out of poverty. There was no room for failure.

When my mother decided to move us out of her mother's house to live on our own, the building that we moved into had no bed. We had to make the floor our bed. That's where I come from. I am Jamaican, and I am my mother's daughter.

My dad was jailed before I was born. He had gone to America for work after my half-sister and I were born, just a week apart. He got caught up with the wrong crowd and had to face the consequences. He was not released from prison until I was three.

Then, he came back to Jamaica to meet me for the first time. But he couldn't stay. A work opportunity presented itself on the Cayman Islands and he gladly took up the offer. After all, his kids had to eat. He visited every year.

My stepfather became the consistent father figure in my life. He would wash, cook, clean, and comb my hair. He took good care of me. I felt that I had two fathers growing up, but I wouldn't be who I am today if it weren't for my mother. She pushed so hard to provide for us.

Jamaica contains two worlds. In one there is a vision of paradise: beautiful beaches, local music, amazing food, and a rich culture. This sometimes masks the poverty and the crime of Jamaica's other world. To avoid becoming a statistic, you have to work hard for what you want. This I learned from my mother.

She was always working. She worked so hard that whenever I asked her to rest it would cause animosity between us. She would tell me that I just didn't understand how many bills she had to pay. "Rest" was never a part of her vocabulary.

Throughout my childhood, she owned a bar, restaurant and grocery shop. But she lost most of it after she had her fourth child. Life changed. Things became harder. It was never easy to get back on her feet.

Today, she still owns the restaurant, but it's much smaller than before. In Jamaica, we would call this a "cookshop." I thank God for my mother's drive because it has equipped me with the self-motivation I need in today's world. I'm always striving to be greater than what I was yesterday.

I got my first real job as a system administrator in May 2010, immediately after I completed my degree in Information Technology. It was a dream come true. I was elated and overwhelmed. I was on top of the world. The three-part interview was tedious, made more challenging by the necessity of competing against men in a field that was dominated by males. It felt good when in the end when I was awarded the position.

Several of my friends were working online and earning American dollars. . . . I thought to myself, I missed something. I could be making money working online, in my own time, doing what I love and doing it from anywhere in the world. Well, it's never too late to start, right?

That's when my life changed. I knew the only direction I could go was up the ladder. There was no stepping down. I was determined to do well for my mom and my younger siblings, to be a role model for them.

I can say I have been doing a damn good job. I was the first to attend college and the first to work in the corporate world. These are accomplishments that I am proud of, but I wanted more.

Discovering Freelancing

IN 2013, WHILE WORKING AS A system administrator, I was introduced to freelancing as a way to work from the comfort of your home.

Of course, I didn't think this could be possible. I thought it must be a scam. I signed up out of reluctant curiosity, but never gave it much thought. Nothing came of it. Then, in 2015, I noticed several of my friends were working online and earning American dollars. It was the very same platform that I had signed up for in 2013. It had not been a scam. I thought to myself, I missed something. I could be making money working online, in my own time, doing what I love, and doing it from anywhere in the world. Well, it's never too late to start, right?

I immediately went online and opened another account. Getting the first job was tough because I had to compete against other more experienced freelancers. It took about three months before I landed my first job, but it was a big job. For a girl living in Jamaica and freelancing on the side, it was quite a prize.

I expected to make three dollars per hour at my first job and instead it was ten dollars! None of my friends were earning that hourly rate. With a limit of 40 hours/week, I had the potential to earn $1,600 USD each month, or approximately $200,000 JMD. That was almost more than my entire monthly salary. My adrenaline started pumping and I got to work immediately.

After working at my day job I would go straight to my online work, putting in my hours and boosting my income. That extra money was reserved for savings, shopping, my family, and traveling. My monthly salary from my day job was enough to pay the bills, but it wasn't enough to do the extras. I absolutely loved going to new places and being able to shop. As you can imagine, shopping was not a part of my childhood. I even bought a new car. I was having fun. I was living a dream, even though I was working two full-time jobs. Still, I wanted more.

> **Unexpected Lifestyle Changes:** Yanique's understanding of how to use technology to work in more lucrative, overseas markets led her to help others. Before long she had started a company training fellow Jamaicans to follow in her footsteps.

Becoming My Own Boss

MY DRIVE AND DESIRE TO DO more, and be more, gave birth to my business, Adept Inventions. I had always wanted to become my own boss.

As a child, my role models did anything they could to make money, anything they could to put food on the table. They hadn't gone to college, and they couldn't find "real" jobs working for someone else. I watched them work, I worked with them, and I learned from their work ethics. I always thought that once I finished high school I would start to hustle or form my own business. I didn't know anything about attending college because I didn't see that possibility growing up. However, we are in the 21st century where we are exposed to the internet and the world beyond our childhood homes. This allowed me to learn about and attend college, but it didn't kill my drive for the hustle—it only made me realize that hustling can be called something else: entrepreneurship.

> **The Best Thing About Work Beyond Wages:**
> "I work for myself rather than helping someone else build their dream for just a salary".

After working online for a few months, my entrepreneurial, philanthropist mind clicked on. Why not spread the word to other Jamaicans about this wonderful opportunity of working online? I will benefit, and they will also benefit. September 11, 2015 was the birth of Adept Inventions Business Process Outsourcing (BPO). Originally, training primarily focused on teaching individuals what it means to be a freelancer and how to get started. For a fee, people could attend training the last Saturday of every month.

When new freelancers contact us they are usually afraid. They fear that they can't do the job, that their clients won't like their work, or that communication will be challenging. More often, though, they are afraid that it is a scam. I am always faced with skepticism and fear. A big part of my job is explaining that freelancing is real and that there is nothing to fear.

This business went well and soon we started to explore the concept of outsourcing, linking our trainees to clients, and ensuring a quality relationship. In order to work directly for Adept Inventions, freelancers have to possess certain qualification and character traits. Our trainees need to have the tenacity and drive to become their own boss because working online takes a lot of discipline. When a client contacts us for a service, we choose from the list of available freelancers based on the skill level needed for the job.

In the midst of working, freelancing, and starting my own business, I also found my husband online. We were married in December 2016. Ours is a wonderful relationship, but it comes with a

unique challenge: my husband lives in America. I
live in Jamaica.

Having a long-distance relationship is never easy
because you have to work twice as hard as the
person who gets to go home to see their partner
every night. We never had enough time. I could not
work all day, freelance all night, start a successful
business, and be a good wife.

The Big Decision

THINGS WEREN'T WORKING. SOMETHING HAD TO
change. I needed to get my business off the
ground. I needed to spend more time with my
husband and not let him feel neglected, So, I
decided to quit my day job. This was a big decision. I was giving up the one sure financial security
I had. I was not sure how my bills would be paid,
but it was worth the risk. My dream was to become
an entrepreneur and to work for myself rather
than helping someone else build their dream for
just a salary.

I left the traditional workforce with a lot of fear
and uncertainty. There were lots of "what–ifs?" My
dad always told me that change is the only thing
that's constant and that I should always take a leap
of faith. After analyzing the pros and the cons, I
realized that there were way more advantages than

there were disadvantages. Looking back, I would definitely make the same decision.

I have no regrets from that choice. Resigning from my job motivated me to go forward and improve.

My Media Appearances

ON JUNE 25, 2017, I GOT an email from one of Jamaica's biggest TV stations. I had been writing to media outlets in Jamaica with a proposal to be on their shows. It was finally happening. I was filled with excitement and nervousness. Within three days I was on National TV for all of Jamaica to see. Then, the phones started to ring. The emails started blowing up. Two weeks later, I was featured in one of Jamaica's major newspapers. I did interviews with an American podcaster and he told me that my episode was the most popular to on his website. He asked me if I was

Top Tips:
"Overcome your fears, and never stop learning. The amount of information online is amazing. You can learn anything you don't know, often for free, using online resources. Also, "gamble with what you can afford to lose, start out small using your free time. Do not quit your job today because it really takes time to build your clientele."

driving traffic to his site. I said not intentionally, but maybe they love my Jamaican accent!

Along with media attention, my idea about training others to be freelancers was starting to really work. More people were signing up. Businesses were calling to ask how they could get a freelancer to work for them. My dream was becoming a reality.

Making the Numbers Work

TODAY I MAKE MY BUDGET WORK through freelancing and through my business.

My primary role on Upwork is Virtual Assistant, but I have done many different types of work including data entry, Graphic Design, English to Jamaican Patois, Email Handling and Social Media Marketer to name a few. The Virtual Assistant category usually covers most of what I have outlined above. Clients like the fact that I am versatile and not just focused on one area.

Adept Inventions has grown significantly over the past two years. We've gone from having seven attendees per workshop to having twenty-five. We have had approximately fifteen workshops since the inception of the business. I currently have three clients and about twenty freelancers on my team.

We have come a long way, but more needs to be done. I am working with a business consultant to find ways to enhance my business and make it grow. Adept Inventions will become a big name. I feel it and I believe it and I am willing to work as hard as possible to make it happen.

Your Success Depends on You!

MY ADVICE TO ANYONE TRYING TO become a freelancer is to get rid of the fear. Life is a gamble: we win some, we lose some. Gamble with what you can afford to lose, start out small using your free time. Do not quit your job today because it takes time to build your clientele.

I also tell freelancers that Google and YouTube are my best friends. Everything I want to know is there. If I am tasked with something I don't know how to do, I ask my "friends" and they show me. They can become your friend too; they are very kind. Do not fear the known or the unknown because both can become your worst enemy. Don't let fear prevent you from starting. You need to start to get to where you want to go.

Name: Aleksandra Kaye

Nationality: Polish

Country of Residence: N/A: Travels full-time

Why She Left the Rat Race: Though Alex had planned to spend time travelling, Brexit became the final push she needed to "let go of the mundane and embrace the life I had always wanted."

CHAPTER FOUR
Brexit: The Final Push
Aleksandra Kaye, *Poland*

IN 2016, MY WORLD SHIFTED. I wasn't alone. As a Polish national who had spent the majority of my life living in the United Kingdom, Brexit hit me hard. My British-centric history made the logistics relatively easy; I had already applied for a UK passport in anticipation of the referendum results. The accompanying feelings were more difficult to resolve. Though my work colleagues were supportive, it felt like the country I had spent most of life in suddenly didn't want me.

My name is Aleksandra and I'm 27 years old. Two years ago, I quit my full-time job to travel the world with my husband, David.

We have been on the road since November 2016. I haven't looked back since. We take odd jobs here and there, but our day-to-day expenses are largely met through working for ourselves. Our lifestyle has allowed me to spend more time with my husband, more quality time with myself, and to experience places and people from all corners of the globe. In some ways, Brexit provided the final push I needed to let go of the mundane and embrace the life I had always wanted.

Going to college inspired my travel plans. I loved university and my degree. I welcomed the independence, the freedom, and the opportunity for a new start after the uneventful high school years.

There was so much going on: lectures by renowned professors, societies to cater to just about any interest, diverse sport clubs, the opportunity to take initiative and organize events. It was fantastic to be surrounded by inspired, intelligent people— their positive energy was infectious. I made amazing friends, with whom I still keep in regular contact with, five years on. It was also at university that I met David, at a canoe club session. We enjoyed each other's company and soon found that we had a lot in common, including a desire to travel the world.

During our first summer together, David and I went interrailing across Europe and discovered that almost every European capital has a cheap campsite. During our second summer, we went to Southeast Asia. David had just completed his degree, while I still had a year left of mine. We agreed that we would travel long-term as soon as I completed my degree, and that David would find a job for a year and wait for me. He ended up taking a job as a teaching assistant, while I worked towards completing my degree.

Nothing ever goes exactly as planned, and I loved university so much that I decided to complete a master's degree before going traveling. I was

---

After completing my master's degree, I decided to find a job. I felt strongly that I needed to become financially independent and reassure my parents that I was going to be alright. I realize now that I was overly concerned about doing what was expected of me.

---

accepted on a course in Transnational History. I was incredibly excited. David was accepted to Cambridge University and found that his one-year PGCE course could lead to a Master of Education if he did an additional year of part-time study. The opportunity seemed too good to pass, so we opted to postpone our travels for two years.

After completing my master's degree, I decided to find a job. I felt strongly that I needed to become financially independent and reassure my parents that I was going to be alright. I realize now that I was overly concerned about doing what was expected of me.

Applying for jobs was a disheartening experience.

I mostly got no response to my applications, or when

Unexpected Lifestyle Changes:
Traveling has taught Alex how little one needs to feel fulfilled. She has become a minimalist, and has never been happier.

I did get a response it was to tell me there were better applicants. It seemed almost all jobs expected years of work experience, which I didn't have. Eventually, I did secure an administrative, full-time, temporary (six-month) job at a university in Cambridge.

The job sounded really good on paper. I was to answer student queries and provide them with clerical support throughout their studies. What I didn't realize when applying was how repetitive the job would be. I had to do administrative tasks on a daily basis that, although important, didn't require much thinking or initiative. Anything remotely more complicated was passed on to senior colleagues, as those of us in entry-level positions were not allowed to deal with those. It made me feel powerless and frustrated. Every morning on my cycle to work I had to tell myself that my job was meaningful, that it was helping someone, that it wasn't a waste of my time.

It was draining though, and I felt trapped. I kept reminding myself that it was only for six months.

My initial six-month contract was extended for another six months. Despite how negatively I felt about the job, I accepted, as David was in the middle of the school year and understandably didn't want to leave his students in the middle of the term. At work, I started counting down the hours until 5pm, pretty much as soon as I got to the office. I needed other activities outside of my career. I signed up for a part-time course where I learned how to teach English as a foreign language. I thought it might be a useful skill to have if we ever did end up taking off and moving to Asia. Later, having come to the conclusion that we had both put on a lot of weight, David and I signed up for some sprint triathlons and began training after work. It gave David an excuse to have some time off from working in the evenings and it was a feel-good activity. After each run, swim, or cycle we felt slightly happier and healthier.

Then one September night after we returned to our flat after a friend's wedding David played me a song on his piano. I protested because it was late and I was concerned about the neighbors, but he was adamant. So, I sat down as he played a song from my favorite childhood film, then got on one knee and asked The Question. Wedding planning took most of our spare time in the year to come and we postponed our travel plans for yet another year while my job continued to extend my contract. We were married in Poland, under two ancient oak trees, in a multilingual ceremony. It was a really special day. Our family and friends from the UK, Poland and all over the world came to celebrate with us. I was incredibly happy.

While things were good in my personal life (despite the continual postponement of our travel plans), trouble was brewing in the country. In May 2015 the Conservative Party returned to power with a surprise majority in the UK general election, and a rashly promised EU referendum became inevitable. I was perfectly happy living in the UK on my Polish passport, but the prospect of the referendum concerned me. Something in the pit of my stomach or perhaps all the negative press migrants got in the British media made me think the vote was going to be to leave the European Union. I decided to apply for British nationality.

The process wasn't simple. Before one can apply for British nationality they need to first apply for permanent residency. The form is 85 pages long and needs to be accompanied by extensive documentation collected over the previous five years.

Getting the form and the documents sorted took weeks. I sent everything off just a few weeks before the referendum—a decision for the UK which would directly affect my life, and one in which I had no say whatsoever.

The day the results were announced was awful. The outcome felt like a punch in the stomach, like the whole country had said *we don't want you here.* I cried at work and my concerned boss suggested I go home early. People at my work were so supportive and kind to me, the token non-Brit in the office. A few months later a sad, blue piece of cardboard came through the post confirming my permanent residency. Another couple of forms, more supporting documents, a test about my knowledge of life in the UK, and a hefty fee later I was invited to swear my allegiance to the Queen. My British passport came through the post just a few days before the prime minister, Theresa May, invoked Article 50, cementing Britain's exit from the European Union.

In summer 2016 we finally decided that we were really, finally, going to go and travel and took steps

> **The Best Thing About Work Beyond Wages:**
> "[My] lifestyle has allowed me to spend more time with my husband, more quality time with myself, and to experience places and people from all corners of the globe."

towards making that a reality. David told his school he was not going to come back after the summer holidays and I rejected my university's offer to relocate to Milton Keynes on a permanent position. In October we packed up all our belongings, moved out of our rented flat, and stayed with David's parents for a month while we finalized our plans.

I think part of the reason we took so long to follow our dreams and why we kept finding reasons to postpone them is because following unconventional dreams is scary. I was worried about quitting my job because, despite everything, it did provide a secure routine and income. David and I had it all sorted: a place to live, steady jobs, being independent. Our plans involved abandoning our security for the unknown. I was rather worried about what our parents were going to think of all this and if we were disappointing them by not pursuing stable careers. It also felt like we were letting our colleagues down by quitting our jobs. Those concerns kept me back for a long time.

I think realizing that we only have one life and that we are the only ones living it gave us the courage to do what we intrinsically knew would make us happy. When we did make the decision and told people about our plans, quite contrary to my expectations everyone was very supportive.

People at work reassured me that I should do what is best for me and they seemed to genuinely mean that. Our parents were and still are very excited about us going after our dreams. We first headed to Norway, just for a few weeks, in the midst of winter. A few years prior we wrote a bucket-list together and one of the top things on it was to see the Northern Lights. We had made several attempts at spotting them over the years, but never successfully. We tried to see them from the UK, venturing as far north as the Orkney Islands and went on a couple of weekend trips to Norway, but we didn't see the elusive, dancing lights once. We realized that to ensure we see them we needed to commit more time towards looking for them. We also realized that Norway was incredibly expensive, so we equipped ourselves with a tent, thick sleeping bags, and layers of thermal clothing and set off with an intention of wild camping.

Camping in arctic Norway in December worked for about a week. It wasn't the cold or the snow, but the thirteen hours of torrential rain which pushed us to book a hotel for a night. The frozen ground did not soak up the rainwater which then just collected under our tent and slowly seeped in through the groundsheet. Everything that wasn't in a drybag was soaked and we couldn't get a fire started to dry things off. With cold and with dampened spirits, we packed up camp and walked in search of a bus.

Eventually, one came and took us to a town with an airport. We hoped to catch a cheap flight or failing that to spend the night at the airport, but that didn't work and we ended up camping in our wet gear on a field by the airport. We were told a coach could take us to our destination at eight in the morning. The coach journey was glorious – the heating was on at full blast and the driver played Christmas songs. When we arrived at Tromsø in the evening we couldn't face a third, cold, wet night so we booked into the cheapest hotel that we could find (which was still mightily expensive) for the night. We also decided to bring forward the rental on the car we initially intended to pick up a week later. The car was cozy, had heated seats, and greatly increased the comfort of the remainder of our Norwegian trip. We did spend a bit more than intended, but sometimes things do not go according to plan and you're faced with additional costs that can't really be avoided. It was worth it though, as we did get to see the northern lights and they were incredible.

After spending the Christmas period with our families, we packed again and headed towards India. Budgeting in India was at the same time easier and harder than in Norway. On one hand, everything in India is significantly cheaper than in Norway, but on the other hand not many services or things had a set price. Negotiation skills are vital and bartering is expected. India is also still very much a cash-based economy, which is completely different to Norway where you can even use your debit or credit card to pay for an unmanned public toilet in the middle of nowhere.

We arrived in India following Prime Minister Narendra Modi's announcement that 500- and 1,000-rupee notes would be taken out of circulation. The effects of that decision were still very much felt. ATMs routinely ran out of cash and when cash was available long queues would form. Most of the ATMs would also only dispense money in 2,000-rupee denominations. Spending the 2,000-rupee note could be a challenge

Top Tip:
Alex's top tip is to work past your fears and take the plunge. "I think part of the reason we took so long to follow our dreams and why we kept finding reasons to postpone them is because following unconventional dreams is scary. Our plans involved abandoning our security for the unknown. Realising that we only have one life and that we are the only ones living it gave us the courage to do what we intrinsically knew would make us happy."

of its own as no one would have change from such a big denomination. However frustrating we found the money situation as travelers, we appreciated how it affected the local people just as profoundly.

We chose trains as our main mode of transport in India. Navigating the country's complicated rail network, we traveled the subcontinent meeting interesting people and learning about India's rich history and assorted cultures. We generally found Indian people very genuine, friendly, and interested in interacting with us. Quite often we would be approached by someone who introduced him or herself and had a little chat with us. This was great. While traveling as a couple is wonderful in many respects it can result in not interacting with as many people. This is partly because in a couple you already have company and someone to talk to, so you are less inclined to approach new people. However, I think strangers also find single people more approachable and less intimidating than they do a couple. The speed that the trains in India travel at, and the resulting long journey times (our train from Kerala to Kolkata took over 46 hours) also encouraged us to make new acquaintances.

We found India to be an incredibly diverse and interesting country with so much to offer. We began our Indian adventure at the Jaipur Literature

Festival, a celebration of knowledge and a fantastic, completely-free week of talks given by some of the world's greatest minds. We ended by celebrating Holi both in Nepal's Kathmandu and, a day later, in India's New Delhi. Upon learning that Jaipur is the Pink City, we decided to also visit Rajasthan's White City—Udaipur, Blue City—Jodhpur and Yellow City—Jaisalmer. It was while we were in Jaisalmer that we received the news we had been accepted for the International Experience Canada (IEC) program. We would go there later in the year.

From the dry, sandy Rajasthan, we headed to the humid, busy Maharashtra and from there to the lush Goa and leafy Kerala in the southwest corner of India. From there we went diagonally across to West Bengal in the opposite corner of India. We also ventured to Assam and Meghalaya in India's so-called "chicken head."

The states and union territories we visited in India felt more different from one another than countries in Europe, yet they unite as one country. It was our first prolonged experience of travel in this part of the world and we began to develop a taste for the heady mix of sightseeing, spicy food, and sights, both natural and historical, that could only be found in India.

We returned to the UK from India in March 2017

with quite depleted wallets. We needed to make some money so we could afford our tickets to Canada and continue our journey. Stationed in David's parents' guestroom David signed up with a

---

Securing freelancing jobs becomes a bit easier the more you do it, as you begin to build up a reputation on the servers. . . . Yet freelancing is unpredictable. Sometimes there are no jobs and at other times there are so many it's hard to manage, but the work is varied and interesting.

---

supply-teacher agency and I registered online with a temping agency. Supply teaching and temping have their merits as you can get work very quickly and you do not have to commit to long-term contracts. After a bit over a month of working, we were able to buy direct flight tickets from London to Vancouver, for just over £200 each. We had to be flexible with our departure date to get such a good price, but it worked out for the best.

Not only did we have more time to replenish our savings, but we were also in the country when Theresa May announced a snap election. This time around I could vote. The election was on the same day as our afternoon flight to Canada, with just enough time to visit the polling station in the morning. It was hard not to feel slight schaden-freude when she lost her majority.

When we first arrived in Vancouver, we based ourselves at an Airbnb for a week to give ourselves time to find and purchase a van or a car. We were looking for a vehicle in which we could live in as we hoped to travel across Canada, camping on Crown Land as we went. Luckily it all went according to plan and we managed to buy Cherry Tom—a red Ford Ranger almost as old as we are—a few days after landing in Canada. Since getting Cherry, we learned a lot more about car mechanics and now know how to change the oil, tires, air filters, lighter fuses, and many more pieces all by ourselves. It's a liberating and reassuring feeling.

Canada is a fantastic place for a nomadic lifestyle. It's never too hard to find a picnic or a camping spot. We travel with everything we need. We have a gas stove, an ice box, and a big water container for our food and drink. We also have a box we call the "kitchen cupboard" full of our cutlery, crockery, pots and pans, and all those other things we need for cooking. We have a laptop and our phones which we use for work on the road and for keeping in contact with our family and friends. There's space at the back of our truck for a mattress and some sleeping bags to sleep in. Our clothes are in a big blue suitcase, our "wardrobe," and all our other clutter goes into a plastic storage box. To make our truck homier and cozier we strung some fairy lights in the back.

Traveling in Canada has also made me realize how many things I do not need and without which I can still lead a very happy existence. We wake up when the daylight or heat drives us out of our truck, we cook our meals at rest stops and backwoods campsites—so our kitchen is in a different place every night—and each city en route becomes a vital stop to take care of essential business, such as doing the laundry or accessing WiFi. We've been without a flat for months now and it really makes me feel that you don't need a house to make a home.

Having replenished our savings while in Cambridge we spent the first month in Canada quite carefree. We were roughly two thirds up our drive across British Columbia, which aptly calls itself the "beautiful province," to Yukon when we checked our finances and came to an uncomfortable realization that we didn't have very much money left at all.

I signed up for some freelancing websites and started sending off applications. A few weeks passed before I got a job offer. Securing freelancing jobs becomes a bit easier the more you do it, as you begin to build up a reputation on the servers. I write articles and translate between Polish and English. Yet freelancing is unpredictable. Sometimes there are no jobs and at other times there are so many it's hard to manage, but the work is varied and interesting. A few weeks ago, I got to translate historical marriage certificates and this week I got to learn about wine regions in the world while researching for a job.

Our lives now are very different from how they were in Cambridge. Although we both work, working on our own schedule instead of 9-to-5 jobs, means David and I now have significantly more time for each other and feel a lot more relaxed. We laugh, share great conversations, and have the energy and motivation to face challenges as they arise. We changed our office and school for a cozy café, a rickety train carriage, a sandy beach, an Airbnb room, or wherever we happen to be.

On our way from Vancouver, across Yukon to Fairbanks in Alaska, we encountered nature like never before in our lives. There are bears and bison walking along the roads in northern British Columbia. The wilderness is humbling and the scenery awe-inspiring. Every province and territory we visited so far has been different and interesting. Throughout the summer months we made our way from midnight sun in the Yukon, through the incredible national parks of the Rockies, across the great plains and past magnificent lakes and forests all the way to Canada's easternmost point in Newfoundland, which feels very close to being back in our British home. I am really glad that I get to experience this journey with David, as it's fantastic to have someone to share my thoughts and observations about new places with, someone to go on hikes with, to try new, exotic foods with, and have all those other experiences, which can be enjoyed alone, but are nicer with a friend.

With the famously-cold Canadian winter around the corner, we now have some big decisions to make. We are exploring options and it's an exciting time. We are hoping to work at a ski resort, benefit from complementary staff ski-passes, and fit in a lot of skiing and snowboarding in our spare time. With no prior experience working in the sector, we realize we might not be hired. If we don't get winter positions, we know we can sustain ourselves by working for ourselves. In its current state Cherry Tom is not suited for temperatures reaching -30°C (-22°F), so if we decide to continue camping through the winter will need to winter-proof it. An alternative would be to find a room or flat to stay in over winter.

Whatever happens and whichever option we follow, having David with me makes me feel safer and more confident that things will work out. He's a calming, reassuring presence.

Now, exactly a year since I quit my 9-to-5 job, reflecting on the decision, I don't regret it at all. I do sometimes miss having a nice flat and living close enough to our families to be able to visit them at short notice. With the technology available today, however, it is possible to be in touch almost wherever we are in the globe. This really helps when missing those from back home. I am also sure that when we do get to see our family and friends next, we will treasure the time all the more. As for the flat, well, a flat can't move. We've managed to make a wonderful, tiny, but cozy home in the back of our Ford Ranger.

Name: Christine Muleme

Nationality: Ugandan

Country of Residence: Uganda

Why She Left the Rat Race: Despite having a successful career, enviable titles, and a steady paycheck, Christine felt isolated and lonely. She wanted the freedom to enjoy her life and spend time with her children, but the rat race wouldn't allow this. "I felt like I was a slave of my education. And I hated it."

CHAPTER FIVE
From Uganda to the Cloud
Christine Muleme, *Uganda*

ANOTHER ROUND OF POLITICAL CHANGES LOOMED. In the 15 years I had worked for my organization, I had come to realize that during the first year after organizational shifts my task was to settle into office and identify allies and foes. It was a time of consolidation. Here is where old-time politicians would lay strategies either to join your camp, or to team up against you. The politics in this organization were based on one question: which region of the country do you come from? Advancement was not necessarily about performance, but about your region of origin.

The office politicians were shrewd. They would try at all costs to have representation on the major policy-making organ, and to strategically plant a representative in the crucial departments of great interest. First, they had to have a representation on the administrative board, the student's council (guild), the vice-chancellor's office, and the accounting and finance office. They knew that if they had a handle on these offices, no matter what, they would be able to drive the institution in their direction. I was a victim of these politics.

As though office politicking was not enough, there was the employee discrimination. In Uganda in the 1990s, to be specific, employees were not categorized in accordance with their abilities but on gender and other discriminatory elements. I had worked in this era where a woman's position was that of a woman.

Prior to the changes that were incorporated in the worker's policy in Uganda in 2000, a woman's salary was irrespective of her position. It was pronounced openly that the woman was not the head of the family, and so she was not entitled to benefits available to men. Recognition in the workplace depended heavily on gender. There was no housing allowance, no utilities allowance, no medication for your members of the family, no education allowance for your children, no this ... and no that.

Although the policy changed in 2000, my organization still wanted to maintain the "man is superior" concept. Women were seen as a burden even though they constituted a minimal number of the entire workforce: less than 10 percent. I therefore wondered why women were seen as such a burden. It did not matter your position. It did not matter your responsibilities. What mattered was that you were a woman. This notion was not palatable to me, but it was how it was.

My organization still wanted to maintain the "man is superior" concept. Women were seen as a burden . . . It did not matter your position. It did not matter your responsibilities. What mattered was that you were a woman. This notion was not palatable to me, but it was how it was.

I had performed very well in senior positions for smaller departments. It was upon this premise that the top appointing organ saw fit to send me to a larger department in hopes of improving its financial reporting image. Office politicking is worse than secular politicking. In most instances, you will not know who your friend is and who your foe is. They used this "good at a distance" or the "isolate him/her" tactic. It worked well. I was suddenly an object of great political interest. The politicians had not fared well since one of their own had performed poorly in financial reporting for three consecutive years. This had led to her demotion and my promotion.

I had to relocate to the offices of this new position since I could not manage to commute, owing to the inconsistency and inherent risks of public transport. It hurt me terribly to separate from my family. The unfair treatment of being identified by "what I was" over "what I could do" was disheartening. My dissatisfaction crystallized when I was reappointed to work as head of the department. Aside from feeling that I lacked the required qualifications to back up that appointment, I had already had enough of titles. It did not excite me anymore. I needed a freer kind of life. This "please madam can you help me out of this challenge" thing did not excite me anymore.

I felt very much isolated and very lonely. The time came when I felt that addressing me by my titles was ridiculous. The titles secured me a juicier paycheck, compared to my peers, but it did not accord me any freedom. I felt like I was a slave of my education. And I hated it.

Inside of me, none of this made sense anymore. I had had enough of the discrimination. The office politicking disgusted me. The guilt of separating from my family weighed heavily on me. One particular incident led me to swear to leave sooner, and not later. While I put in my all to ensure efficiency at my job, I had sacrificed my children's childhood experiences and happiness. I had left my baby of four years in a boarding school to have sufficient time to be efficient at work. Sometimes I would even miss the "parents visiting day", which came only once every thirteen weeks. Why? Our office was not highly automated and it was busy. Sometimes there were work backlogs that you had to meet. This time around, I was working in the disbursements office. This entailed making sure that all of the employee's reports were captured and placed into the system before you could consider the payroll complete. The employee's accounts had to be up-to-date with all credits and debits for the month entered. Sometimes these reports were delayed which necessitated working until late in the night to ensure that all reports were in the accounting system.

With this confusion, I had a friend that acted like a real sister. She voluntarily took over my motherly roles. She escorted my children to school and visited them on those special visiting days. She would take them to the hospital in case of sickness. My husband was very supportive, but our children needed a female figure in their lives. So, this friend-turned-sister was a true godsend.

Then the unthinkable happened. Her husband died after a long illness. Since she is a lone child herself, and our relationship had grown to be like family, I was devastated.

He died near the end of the month. Because I knew of the illness, I had worked tirelessly for weeks to ensure that everything was in place. I entered all the debit and credit reports into the employees' accounts to ensure completeness. In fact, that very night, I stayed at the office until 2 am to confirm that all records were entered, and that the payroll was ready for the business manager's signature. After preparing everything, I made printouts, filed them, prepared the checks, and delivered them to the business manager's desk for approval the following day. Since he was away, I informed my immediate supervisor and asked for permission to go and be there for my sister during this time of grief. The following morning, I took the first public taxi at 5 am to be with the mourners and to prepare to attend the burial, which was a long distance from my workplace.

As I traveled to the burial place, my immediate supervisor called my mobile number asking where I was. I reminded her that I was going to attend the burial of the husband of "the only person that has been there for my children." She commanded me to "come back immediately." I explained to her that I had already traveled a great distance, and even if I stopped immediately and turned back, it would be late in the evening by the time I reached the office. She ignored all my pleas. This time it was a command: "Come back immediately."

The Best Thing About Work Beyond Wages: In addition to the freedom to spend her time how she sees fit, Christine has become more confident and is proud to have developed an international clientele that is more than happy with her work. "It is more satisfying to know that it does not matter where I am; the fact that I can deliver quality work and compete on a global platform is invigorating."

I felt all the bitterness flow into my blood. I became determined to leave. Not just to find another job, but to find a freer kind of life. It was security vs. freedom, more socialization, and a fulfilled family life. I hated feeling as if I were a slave to my work, and a stranger to my very loved ones.

With the decision to leave on top of my to-do list, I had one big problem. Unemployment is a global challenge, although sometimes the woman may have better chances than the husband. This was my situation. I was supporting the family. I wondered how we would maintain the children in school. With the first girl in high school, and the baby in elementary school, how could we support our children's education with only one source of income?

My contribution to the family finances was crucial. In 2000, when the policy of allowing women benefits other than salary changed, I had ensured that I was considered for allowances. How could my family continue without my income and without these allowances?

It took me about six months to decide how to quit and to think about what would happen to my children if things didn't go well. I was not sure of my decision. This was a dragon to slay for sure. I had choices to make. I knew that things would not be the same, but I could not consider being in my job for another single moment. I knew inside of me that after a year or two of struggling and getting used to the outside world, I would be able to find my financial footing.

Surviving until then was going to be a big challenge. I had a small garden, and we had managed to build our own house. So, we would not worry so much about money for residential rent. I knew that we would have enough food to take us through a considerable part of the year. But could I get used to the new circumstances? What about other needs that required physical cash?

Some people see only the titles that precede your name, and never the pain you go through. Many of my high school friends had not seen the same corporate advancement that I had attained. Despite my titles, I envied them because they had the freedom to do what they wanted. I saw that they had complete control over their lives. I felt that I missed this kind of life.

I sat down and did the mathematics. I calculated the amount of money I was making per month and narrowed it to per day. And I convinced myself that if I could make the same during my first year, I would not feel the burden so much. But how?

I determined that with my handicraft I might be able to make the same amount of money to meet my day-to-day needs. I felt that with my creativity, I would be able to make enough through crafts production to be able to meet my basic needs. But I needed to be sure before I could quit.

The craft business was a struggle. I used to make gift pieces out of beadwork, encrypted with custom messages. They turned out to be really beautiful. I made mosaics out of ordinary things like beans, maize seeds, and beads. It was time-consuming and tiresome, but it could grant me survival of some sort. Sometimes I would get bigger orders for sculptures. This would earn me up to six figures in UGX, or three figures in USD. I enjoyed it, but it brought in very little income and was inconsistent. It was not enough.

> **Top Tip:**
> Never stop searching for opportunities. There are more options than most people know. "I think that more people would be able to take advantage of international freelancing if they only knew the opportunities that existed."

I had amassed close to 20 years of relying on the security of a paycheck. Though it was not very substantial, it always came. I was scared of what would happen with that security gone.

I started weighing my priorities. Job or family? One day I asked myself a question: "Shall I be able to rewind the clock and recover this lost time with my children? Will these children have a childhood memory with a mother that exists in title only?"

As I ranked my priorities, I decided on an exit route. Whatever the results, I had to move. It was time to go. I did not have many savings from my full-time job and the crafts business would not be enough. However, in the city, freelance secretarial services could put food on the table. I offered my resignation.

My superiors could not imagine it. They thought I had landed a better job. My board chairman and immediate supervisor was put to task to find out where else I had found a job. They had people follow me to find out where I was working. They were surprised that I had left. It is not common for a person to simply leave a job without a proper destination. All efforts to woo me back were fruitless. I was determined.

I rented an office room within a college campus. Having left my corporate job with only a computer and a brain, I humbled myself by offering secretarial services to college students. With the wealth of customer care I had attained in the managerial position of my corporate job, I attained the favor of the students. This particular college consists of students from poor backgrounds—orphans, single-parent children, and people who had not fared well academically. They usually referred to me as "mom." Many were training to be teachers.

For their course, they were required to make creative craft pieces, models, and many other handiwork projects. As luck would have it, I had a friend who worked for an expatriate family, who were leaving

Uganda and selling many of their things. My friend asked me whether I would buy some used children's books and other more sophisticated education materials. I agreed. Little did I know that this would be a real asset in the business.

With these books and other education materials, I had a crude idea of what these students wanted in terms of handiworks. This turned out to be a business opportunity for me, with the students as my main clients.

This business flourished much more than the secretarial business. With the two, I was able to make up for the lost income from my corporate job. It was very tiresome, though, and I always felt I could do something much better. The craft business was about the money, and money it brought in! At least enough to put food on the table, and to meet our basic needs.

My life was multitasking. I had made this change for more time with my family but I was working tirelessly at what felt like two full-time jobs. I needed a job that paid better. I started to pursue online freelancing alongside the secretarial and craft business.

My first days of freelancing were not without challenges. I knew there were better opportunities online, but I had only myself to consult. No one I knew made money online. I kept working in crafts and as a secretary to keep my children in school, while also becoming more acquainted with how I could offer services online. I had

---

I have worked with people from diverse backgrounds from the comfort of my home. It does not matter where I am—the fact that I can deliver quality work and compete on a global platform is invigorating, and the thought of being identified by probable clients from all over the world is gratifying.

---

started training in copywriting, but I had not gone far. I settled in the comfort of the skills that I already possessed. Persistent search and focus made me put my profile on an online job platform. After a few months, and several contracts, I was identified as a "Rising Talent." This one move turned on the light bulb.

After one week of getting this reconigtion, I received an invitation for a simple app localization job. I actively provided unsolicited suggestions to my client to help make this project a success. After successful completion of the first contract, one month later, she sent me a direct offer for a longer-term project. I got other short-term, one-time projects and performed very well. I received 5-star ratings on all of those projects. After three months of landing my first online project, I rose to the Top-Rated status, raised my profile rate, and landed other projects, from all around the world. The rates I was able to secure were much higher than I had been able to access in the local Ugandan market.

I have since diversified and landed another, bigger contract with a more established client through LinkedIn. I have worked with this client for the past six months, and they are contemplating giving me bigger responsibilities.

I have made it.

Today, I am living a more satisfying life. I can visit my children at school. I choose who to work for, and when to work.

I have worked with people from diverse back-grounds from the comfort of my home. It does not matter where I am—the fact that I can deliver quality work and compete on a global platform is invigorating, and the thought of being identified by probable clients from all over the world is gratifying.

My friends often ask what I am doing. When I tell them I am offering services in the cloud, they wonder how I am able to do this. I think that more people would be able to take advantage of international freelancing if they only knew the opportunities that existed.

Name: Xionary Guerrero

Nationality: Venezuelan

Country of Residence: Argentina

Why She Left the Rat Race: Xionary left the rat race out of necessity: to survive an economic recession. "My country crumbled . . . It was chaos. Lack of products became a rule . . . The dollar became a standard we could not attain, a relic, a reminder of what stable money is and what it can do." When Xionary realized she could earn US dollars online, everything changed.

CHAPTER SIX
Escaping Dictatorship and Making My Way
Xionary Guerrero, *Venezuela*

IN 2013, LIFE WAS GOOD. I had spent years working, settling down, and crafting a life for myself. Even though my job wasn't exciting or fulfilling, I was happy overall. My husband and I had savings and owned a safe, stable home. We were ready for more. We were ready to have a family. I became pregnant and fell in love with my belly. Those first months were beautiful.

It was not to last. Something was happening in my country that would stop all my plans.

My name is Xionary and I am Venezuelan born and raised. I studied modern languages in school and was working full-time as an English teacher before I even graduated. I am a free-spirit, but I was trained and configured to work a 9-to-5 job. I needed money and I needed a good CV. By 24 I was married, and by 26 I had been through several long-term, full-time jobs related to education.

I felt something wasn't right. Is this what I was meant to do?

Although I love teaching languages, I never fit into the teacher mold. I never felt like one of the teachers with the teacher's staff. I struggled to fit in, trading my sneakers for high heels. By 2012, I was overworked, overweight, and exhausted. I decided to end my teaching career.

I moved to a big company in Venezuela and was earning around five times the minimum wage, but it wasn't *living* for me. I tried another career as a bilingual assistant, which was good at the beginning because I liked what I was doing, but I wasn't *there* yet (you know, the *right* place). I turned to my family and became joyfully pregnant.

Then my country crumbled.

Venezuela became the country with high inflation. It was chaos. Lack of products became a rule. We were always standing in long lines to purchase even the most basic of things. The dollar became a standard we could not attain—it became a relic, a reminder of what stable money is and what it can do. The dollar was not obtainable for the ordinary citizen. It happened fast, and it was ruthless. It was 2014, the year everyone started to fall apart in my country. The fall hasn't stopped since. We are so far down the rabbit hole.

So there I was, with a baby about to be born in a country full of disease and no medicine, a country with hyperinflation, a country with daily blackouts and no water service, a country with no food, no

---

There I was, with a baby about to be born in a country full of disease and no medicine, a country with hyperinflation, a country with daily blackouts and no water service, a country with no food, no democracy, and no freedom. There was no future for me or my son. I was scared and shocked.

---

democracy, and no freedom. There was no future for me or my son. I was scared and shocked.

My husband is a graphic designer. He loves working for himself and he has always been a part-time freelancer. One day we received a visit from one of his clients who told us about freelancing sites and payment methods such as Payoneer and PayPal. I was amazed. I thought it could not be real, and I wondered: how can I make dollars? How can a Venezuelan person earn her own dollar without government control?

I went for it and made a profile. It did not work at first. For months there was no answer, so I decided to make a video. I made the video for a Chinese website who was looking for teachers. It was a very simple low-resolution video, but results exceeded my expectations. Using the video, I found four students: Adrian from Poland, Nox from Israel, Sara from Italy, and Mostafa from Turkey. I had done it! I was teaching online for 12 hours per week at a rate of $2 USD per hour. Twenty-four dollars per week might not seem much, but in Venezuela that is a lot of money. I was able to buy everything for my baby, pay a clinic where I could give birth, and buy all the things we needed.

Unexpected Lifestyle Changes: In addition to maintaining a lifestyle that would have been impossible working for local wages in Argentina, Xionary can now schedule her work around her life. The time spent with her young son and the ability to accomplish other life goals alongside a full-time workweek is invaluable.

On January 27th, 2015 my baby was born. He has been beautiful since day one, that smell, that nose. I love him. When I got back home with my newborn, I knew I wasn't going to go back to work. I wasn't going to leave my baby and let other people experience all his firsts instead of me, but how could I stop working in a country whose economy is sinking?

Every day there were new, higher prices for everything. Freelancing became a life or death choice. I never saw myself as a stay-at-home mom, but I did not want to miss a thing. I also had to provide. I wanted to provide well, which was impossible with the economic situation we were living through in our country. I wanted to provide more than money, too. I wanted to teach him what freedom and happiness meant by being an example of it. There were so many things that I wanted to accomplish but I was very far away from doing anything at that time.

The idea of leaving the country started to come into our heads. We had blackouts every day and the internet wasn't very good (1mb speed). I started to apply for online work during my maternity leave and I got my first virtual assistant job. I was doing calls and emails for 20 hours per week for a real estate company. I was making $60 USD per week, plus income from teaching my four students, so I decided to quit my job for good.

I was working 35 hours per week and the money I was making was enough to live in Venezuela with basic things. But our country was sinking rapidly. We had to leave and we had to save money. Our only other option was to find a job we could do anywhere and still be sustainable.

I started applying for full-time teaching jobs. I did many interviews and got a job with an online school in Vietnam as a full-time teacher for $500 USD per month. I was happy, overjoyed. But it did not last long. During my first week, a new series of blackouts happened in my city and that affected the internet. I spent three days without the internet (as did the whole city) and when I got it back, I had been removed from the teaching schedule. I was sad and frustrated. I had lost a big opportunity.

Nevertheless, giving up has never been an option for me so I started applying for translation and interpreter jobs. I got another job as an online phone interpreter. In this particular task, I had to translate live calls. It didn't have a fixed scheduled so it fit me perfectly at the time. I still had my two other jobs, so I saved around 300 USD and decided to leave the country with my husband and son.

On March 6th, 2016 we left Venezuela by bus. We crossed the border with 300 USD and three jobs that brought in a monthly income of 400 USD. We arrived in Bogotá, Colombia and our journey began anew. We arrived with little money. In Venezuela, the electricity and internet service had not been very good and I couldn't work as much as I had wanted.

When I arrived in Bogota, I realized the amount of money my husband and I were making would barely support us, as exchange rates in Venezuela are very different. We needed to make better online profits. We even thought about looking for a 9-to-5 job. I actually found a full-time job, and got hired, but when I got home, I felt depressed. I had failed myself. It was never my idea to merely survive. Having to deal with schedules, co-workers, and dress codes was even more depressing. Having to leave my little son at a daycare was not part of my dream either.

> **The Best Thing About Work Beyond Wages:**
> "I have been able to leave a dictatorship behind, taking my young son with me to a place that offered far more opportunities, freedom, and security. . . . I am part of the new wave, a new lifestyle, a new way of working: remote online work."

We did not have any family in Colombia and leaving my son at such a young age (1-year-old) at a daycare wasn't the best option for me. He had just left his whole country, his own house, his own family behind, and moreover he was going to stay away from me in this immigration process. So I called my job and told them I wasn't a good fit. I went back to online working and applying for better jobs.

In order to get my dream clients, I decided to do every free online course related to virtual assistant services. I used HubSpot and Udemy and many portals like that. About four months into our move I finally got one of my first long-term, nearly full-time clients. I worked for this office over 30 hours a week. With this new office work in addition to my other clients my income finally became steady.

Our journey was not over. We realized that we needed a visa to be able to stay as legal residents in Colombia. Visa options did not include freelancing, so once again we had to move. Once again (but now with more experience) we were thinking about where we could live, and about how much money we would need to get there. We had barely two months to save money and leave. It was less time than people usually have to decide about where to immigrate. We reviewed the wages of different countries, travel tickets prices, and visa opportunities for freelancers in countries near us, because we only had enough money to travel by bus. After a very extensive list of pros and cons we made a decision: Quito, Ecuador would be our next destination.

We arrived in Quito on September 27th, 2016. Venezuela, my own country, was sinking even deeper, and my family back home was struggling. I had left a second country and I was desperate to make it work. In Ecuador, I started as an established virtual assistant. I had a full schedule of work, but I was determined to learn more and offer more to my clients. I signed up

for my first online postgraduate course to be an entrepreneur. I learned a lot about how to manage my time,
how to create a project to sell, how to create offers, and
to create a business plan
for my virtual assistant
project. This course gave
me a direction. I would
recommend it to anyone.
Afterwards, I felt I
needed to learn more so
I signed up for a social

> **Top Tip:**
> "The most valuable
> thing I've learned is that
> I am more disciplined,
> driven, and goal
> achieving than I ever
> knew. You are, too."

media management diploma. I studied for 6 months
to get it. I did it all online while working 40 hours a
week and raising my son (with no help because all
my family is in Venezuela). Being able to care for
your child at home is one of the many advantages of
quitting a 9-to-5 job. I was able to arrange my
schedule around my daily life, including my son. I
organized myself so I could take my son to school,
exercise, and work 40 to 45 hours per week without
having to quit my actual life.

Many people are scared to leave behind a "secure
job" because of the benefits, but for me the benefits
were not enough. I might have had a steady income,
but I was unable to make more money than that
steady income if I needed it. Right now, I make the
money I need. If I need more money, I work more

or I study more and I am able to provide another service with a higher pay rate. I am not limited.

Starting might be slow, but when you build yourself an online reputation work never stops. I haven't stopped working since 2015. I have been able to leave a dictatorship behind. I have been able to take my young son with me to a place that offered far more opportunities, freedom, and security. I have been able to share many intimate moments with him and provide for him. At the same time, I am part of the new wave, a new lifestyle, a new way of working: remote online work. I connect with people all over the world, I learn about new cultures and new ways of working. I offer services, but I also feel globalization is teaching me how important it is to be connected worldwide.

I feel like I am at my best every day and the goals keep growing and growing. I use a second language, learn, study, and tackle new tasks every day. I don't have a boss or any of the problems that come with one. Instead, I have clients and I get to choose whether I continue working with them. I am not limited or stuck. I am open to growing on my own terms.

The most valuable thing I've learned is that I am more disciplined, driven, and goal-focused than I ever knew. I rely on my reputation to get clients, so I must work hard and be truly excellent all the time. As I have succeeded, my self-esteem has grown so much. The feeling you get when someone from a foreign country loves your work and values your services is very gratifying.

I feel my professional career is just starting and it will grow even more. I just signed up for a digital marketing diploma. Studying is never off the table for me and I am making around four times the Ecuadorian minimum wage per month. Along with my family, I am planning to move again to another country, this time Argentina. I already know people there that I met as clients and I am sure Argentina is a rising market that will open doors and offer great opportunities.

I am a better person now. I am happier, and I have time for my son. I can travel and see the world and I am not underpaid. This life has taught me a new configuration and I feel free. Above all, I was able to escape the dictatorship and hardships in my country. This is my life, this is the future, and I hope everyone can share this kind of freedom and happiness in their work. I know they can. It only takes a small change in mindset and a desire to live your own life.

Name: Klara C. Racpan

Nationality: Filipina

Country of Residence: Colombia

Why She Left the Rat Race: Klara found herself living
through each day without really enjoying the moments.
Her life felt monotonous and devoid of passion. A
three-week holiday taught her that it didn't need to be
this way, and she set about creating a life that would
excite her.

CHAPTER SEVEN
Veering Off the Tracks
Klara C. Racpan, *Philippines*

I FIGURED IT WAS A GOOD time to break the news. On a typical humid Sunday morning in my household, I leaned my head against the wall as I watched my parents debate about a local volleyball match on television. "Oh, by the way, I'm leaving for South America next week and I'll be there for six months," I told my parents nonchalantly. Aghast and incredulous, they stared at me blankly. At twenty-seven, it was my first time to leave home, and to live in a foreign country thousands of miles away, where I knew no one.

I almost gave my parents a heart attack that day.

I'm lucky to have parents who tolerate such an adventurous daughter. I have been traveling now for seven years. Since my first adventure in Colombia, I have seen various countries, collected fascinating stories, and met numerous individuals along the way.

I traveled a lot albeit for short stints as I had to keep a day job. I hopped from one place to another, but always with a feeling of haste as I needed to go back home for work. I knew that I was tied to my job but chose to ignore it. I despised my dependence but dared not question it as it provided for my needs. Instead, I would console myself with the fact that at least I was able to go on escapades, despite their brevity.

I was in the rat race for eight years. I had fun for a while but eventually got tired of it. . . . But at the end of the day, I felt like there was something lacking. I felt as if I was always reaching for something I couldn't describe. My days were monotonous, forced, and inauthentic. I would get up in the morning only to look forward to the end of my day. Pathetic, I thought. But that was the life expected of me. And so, like a living zombie, I shoved my thoughts aside and deluded myself into believing this was a life of normalcy.

I am from the Philippines, a tropical country in Southeast Asia where the people are as warm as the weather. I grew up in a bustling and diverse metropolis called Manila. I studied at a prestigious university and earned a degree in international relations which I finished in three years. Thereafter, I worked for a multinational company and, after several years, transferred to a few more.

Like everyone else, I was expected to follow social norms. After graduation, I needed to find and keep a job at a major corporation. I was supposed to find a company, rise up the ranks, and stick with it until retirement. While managing a stressful but lucrative career, I was to find a loving, caring, and responsible husband. After marriage, I should be able to bear a child, no later than my mid-thirties lest my eggs dry up. While juggling a career and a family, I should also be able to surround myself with the material comforts of a big house and a flashy car that would establish my financial stability and thus my social status.

I tried to fulfill my social duties. I was in the rat race for eight years. I had fun for a while but eventually got tired of it. Perhaps hoping for a change in disposition, I transferred to different companies and tried jobs in various industries. I was grateful for the experiences and realizations each new job brought. I learned a lot and made lasting friendships.

But at the end of the day, I felt like there was something lacking. I felt as if I was always reaching for something I couldn't describe. My days were monotonous, forced, and inauthentic. I would get up in the morning only to look forward to the end of my day. Pathetic, I thought. But that was the life expected of me. And so, like a living zombie, I shoved my thoughts aside and deluded myself into believing this was a life of normalcy. At that time, I had planned a three-week holiday in Asia and Australia so I decided to just suck it up.

Unexpected Lifestyle Changes: Klara has found that new places, people, and discoveries keep her on her toes, growing and evolving as a person. She celebrates each experience and their accompanying revelations.

Little did I know that my trip would be my impetus to change.

I was ecstatic to get a break from the dreary existence I had been enduring. I felt invigorated and invincible exploring different cities. I went to famous beaches in Australia to soak up the sun, culture, and waves. I wandered aimlessly around graffiti-filled streets and narrow alleyways in Melbourne. I explored hole-in-the-wall restaurants in Sydney, surprised to be delighted by the contrasting and decadent flavors. I visited friends, relatives, and acquaintances. I got a glimpse of their lives, their struggles, and their opportunities. I wanted something like that for myself. Back home, it is common for Filipinos to leave their families in search of better opportunities abroad. They leave as a form of sacrifice in exchange for providing a better and comfortable life for their families. They slave away in their jobs in order to be surrounded by material comforts. They build a house, purchase a car, dress with branded clothing, and send savings to their relatives back home. They supply their families with money and possessions in lieu of their physical presence.

Maybe money can buy happiness after all, I thought, as I watched my friends who had left the Philippines proudly showcase their accomplishments. They seemed content, happy, and secure. Yet, I wondered if their lives were really better away from home. Pondering the definitions of successful living, I toyed with the idea of moving to a different country. Perhaps my life would improve too if I moved overseas. I contemplated my future as I sat and waited. Amidst the questions in my mind, I heard a woman call out my flight. I stood up, hesitantly dragged myself out of my head, and walked to the gate. Alas, my time in Australia has come to an end. I boarded the plane and set off for Asia.

Upon landing, I was greeted by hot, humid air, overwhelming and suffocating me. I grew up in a tropical country, so I am used to the warm weather, but I wasn't prepared for the sun's scorching rays or the humidity. On the verge of exasperation, I took a deep breath to calm myself. I had about a week left in my holiday, so I convinced myself that nothing was going to dampen my spirits. I confidently walked out the glass paneled airport doors and looked forward to a new adventure as I now embraced Singapore.

It wasn't my first time in the country, but I saw a different side of it by joining a bicycle tour around the city. After five hours of non-stop pedaling, my legs betrayed me but my faith in humankind was restored. During the tour, I met a Chilean guy and a couple of German girls who patiently waited for me as I navigated the city's paved roads. They cheered me on and pedaled patiently by my side to ensure that I stayed with the group. I was embarrassed for holding them back yet humbled by their willingness to assist me.

This was common in my culture. People would always go out of their way to help, but I wasn't used to seeing that characteristic from other nationalities. I realized then how much people are willing to assist if you have the courage to ask for it. As it turns out, it wasn't just inherent in my culture—it was a personality trait that could be found around the world. Funny how we categorize ourselves and each other based on our citizenship. We cling to our nationalities assuming we're somehow unique. Yet when stripped to the core, we find that inside, we are all the same. We hold the same beliefs, biological composition, and behavioral patterns. I mused over this new awareness as I boarded the bus to Kuala Lumpur.

The Best Thing About Work Beyond Wages: "I have been able to create a life that excites me."

Out of spontaneity, I decided to visit an acquaintance I met in Australia. I boarded the bus amazed at the idea of staying with someone I had only talked with for an hour. Smiling to myself, I welcomed the uncertainty and looked forward to another journey. Ten hours later, exhausted from the long drive, I got off the bus with my gracious host nowhere in sight. This should be interesting, I thought.

Welcome to Malaysia.

Fortunately, we found each other. And I found a taste for Malaysian cuisine. I ate my way through the entire trip. I slurped on viciously spicy noodles that brought me to the brink of tears. I inhaled servings of the famous Nasi Lemak with spoonfuls of spicy sambal chili sauce. I scarfed down and reeked of durian, a delicious fruit with a deceptively pungent aroma akin to an amalgamation of damp feet and rotten onions.

My tummy was full and so was my heart. I was overwhelmed with gratitude for the kindness and warm hospitality that was bestowed upon me. Through a leap of faith, I visited a stranger in a foreign country where I knew no one and expected nothing. In turn, I was welcomed with so much openness and generosity. Though I stayed only for a few days, I felt as if I had been with a longtime friend. I carried with me memories of our friendship and looked forward to creating more upon my return. I visited Malaysia with the intention of meeting a stranger but came home with a newfound sister. High from my trip, I giddily hopped on the plane back to the Philippines and prepared to face my reality.

A week later, I quit my job.

I can't pinpoint a specific reason for leaving everything behind. Maybe I wanted to get away from the mundaneness of my world. Maybe I wanted to find meaning. Maybe I craved the excitement of adjusting to a new culture. Maybe I wanted to challenge myself. Maybe I wanted to meet new people who challenged my beliefs. Maybe I wanted to see the world as it really is and not as a photograph taken through a lens. Perhaps, it was all that, or none of it.

I suppose I left because I wanted to entertain the idea of possibilities. I wanted to see if I had the courage to venture into the uncertainty of a new environment. I wanted to see if I could trust myself enough to plan as I traveled and to open myself up to opportunities as they arose. I wanted to see if I could challenge my imagination to create a life that would excite me. I wanted to see if I could push my limitations to the point of invincibility.

I grew up instilled with the knowledge of what was safe and normal, and of the threats beyond these boundaries. Out of fear, I only dealt with experiences that were within my comfort zone. Yet in the back of my mind, I wondered about the reality of the dangers of society and culture that my parents had warned me about. Perhaps they were real dangers, or maybe they were only an illusion, designed to trap me in my fears. Whatever they were, I was ready to find out.

I broke the news to my family, easily overshadowing my parent's volleyball game, and found myself in South America shortly thereafter

Equador was the perfect place to confront my fears. It was a land of contrasts and misconceptions—good and bad, secure and dangerous, kind and ruthless. Little did I know that along with my own uncertainties, I would have to deal with the doubts of locals, relatives, friends, and even my fellow travelers! I left my country to rid myself of anxieties but ironically, I found more as I pursued my adventure. I met locals who projected their fears and angst from their country's dark history. I encountered well-meaning individuals who warned me of the dangers that lurked behind closed doors. I listened to travelers who exuded paranoia and skepticism as they shared their stories of misfortune. I pacified my relatives who constantly feared for my life, imagining the worst for me.

I understood the reasons behind their doubts. Our imaginations can run wild, sometimes to our detriment. Compounded by stories from the media, we create a world of fear, danger, and distrust. We aggravate our fears by reminiscing and perpetuating stories of hardship and distress we hear from others. And perhaps as a form of vindication, we search, remember, and share stories to prove exactly how dangerous the world is.

But I was stubborn. I was also determined to refute that way of thinking and to replace it with one of adventure and opportunities.

After touring Ecuador, I decided to go to Colombia on a whim. I booked a ticket knowing that I would be entering a country notorious for drug use (I knew this thanks to a television series called *Narcos*). Then again, the Philippines has its share of contraband, so I figured I should feel right at home.

I arrived at ten in the evening in El Dorado International Airport. Joining the crowd, I walked nervously towards immigration. I was traveling like any other legal tourist on vacation, free of crime and guilt, but I felt nervous and uneasy. I suppose it was the general vibe of haste and suspicion that made me uncomfortable as officers determined the motives of hundreds of individuals crossing their border. I approached a stern looking immigration officer and held my breath as she interrogated me about my stay. After a long pause, which seemed like an eternity, I heard a loud thump on the table. With an impassive expression, she looked into my eyes, almost piercing into my soul as she blurted out: "Enjoy your stay in Colombia." She bequeathed my passport with her stamp of approval and sent me off. I took my passport with a smile and thanked her as I meticulously examined the stamp. I hurriedly walked towards the gate and let out a sigh of relief.

In contrast to the warm, friendly, and energetic locals—nothing like the immigration officers at the airport—the weather in Bogotá was, at first, cold, damp, and gloomy. When the weather improved, it was lively yet tranquil, safe yet uneasy, and secretive yet open. It had its charm, but after a week in the city, I was prepared to move on. As fate would have it, I met a man with whom I would share an inexplicable bond.

Top Tip:
"Embrace possibilities, vastness, and freedom."

It was serendipity.

A gentleman in every aspect, he had a compassionate soul and a generous heart. He was adorably considerate with a thoughtful and caring demeanor. He was quick-witted and intelligent, which resulted in endless discussions on a myriad of topics for days on end. He was endearingly funny, bringing me to the brink of tears as I laughed uncontrollably at his effortless remarks. He was easy to be around, uncomplicated and unassuming.

What started with an innocuous smile led to nights of endless conversations and playful banter. Playfulness then led to comfortingly tight hugs and infinite kisses. Our days were filled with a sense of security, companionship, and bliss. We traveled for a while—explored cobblestone roads, underground local scenes, and breathtaking landscapes. We made new friends, drank, and hung out with locals and fellow travelers. We sampled flavorful dishes and gushed at their freshness and taste. We teased and pushed with lighthearted tenderness, unconsciously bringing out the best in each other. Ours was a relationship with reciprocated ease and openness. It was akin to finding a puzzle piece that fit perfectly into its mold—snug, natural, and secure. Though not bound by the length of time, we felt comfortable enough to be vulnerable, letting go of facades without fear of judgment. We showed each other the most genuine aspects of ourselves and were greeted in return with full acceptance.

But every romantic story must have its end.

He was set to return to his country to start anew. Excited for new beginnings but sad to leave, he packed his bags as he prepared to begin another phase of his life. We both moved on literally and figuratively, hoping and knowing that we would find each other again.

To bid him farewell, I wrote: "I will miss you and if you ever miss me too, just look at the stars. They will remind you that although I am physically distant, I am never far away." I continued with my journey, alone, but not lonely.

I was traveling by myself, but I constantly met a lot of fellow wandering souls. Out of curiosity, I would ask them if they liked traveling alone or with a companion. The resounding answer was a preference for traveling alone. Like me, they were able to talk to anyone they met and were able do anything

---

I have had my share of doubts, fears, disappointments, and misfortunes. I have felt vulnerable, homesick, jaded, and disheartened. Despite it all, I chose to focus on the aspects of my journey which have kindled a sense of childlike wonder within me. I pondered on wisdom, learning, and progress. I contemplated the impact of change, movement, and growth on my life. I focused on journeys, discoveries, and adventures. . . . I questioned, I leaped, and I soared.

---

they wanted without the constraints of a partner. I understood their perspective on independence and shared the sentiment, yet I also saw value in company, and having someone with whom you could share experiences.

I grew up in a culture where independence meant isolation. All throughout my life, I was surrounded by people regardless of where I went or what I did. I lived with my siblings and parents. I wandered and explored with friends and relatives whenever I traveled. I was never alone. Although I was free to decide and act for my benefit, I always considered their needs. At some point, it did feel stifling to always think of other people's needs and wants, but at the same time, I did miss them when I was away.

As I compared the similarities of my life with those I met, I saw irony in the longing for both isolation and inclusion. The people I met, like me, ran away when we felt smothered by the presence of others, yet we longed for it when alone. It's not that we wish to be alone but perhaps we seek companions who will allow us an ultimate and full expression of ourselves. We yearn for independence in all aspects of our lives—from the freedom to decide, to the freedom to act on impulses, and to bond with others. For when we feel limitless, we become the best version of ourselves.

As I sat on a wooden park bench in Bogotá, I pondered the idea of freedom in relationships. I watched people go about their lives, oblivious to my amused gaze. I saw a group of boys dancing and clapping, couples hugging and kissing, students chatting and laughing. I marveled at the interactions that surrounded me as I considered my isolation from family and friends.

I remembered an interesting conversation with a guy I met at a yoga farm. "Do you have many friends?" he asked me. To which I replied, "Yes! I have many and you are my friend too!" Surprised at my response, he retorted, "But I have not known you for long. The people I consider friends are those I see, talk to every day, and ask about my life." Taken aback, I looked at him as I thought about the idea of friendship.

I have friends from all over the globe with whom I have established a lasting connection. I do not see or communicate with them regularly, but our bonds are never extinguished. I have met strangers with whom I felt instantaneous ease and comfort. I have a family with whom I share a bond that traverses time and territories. Different circumstances, timelines, and distances, and yet they are all valuable to me. His words echoed in my head as I thought about its veracity. "What defines the quality of our relationships," I asked myself as I watched the world go by.

I have been living in Colombia for a few months now, working with the local government to help improve tourism in the country. I agreed to participate initially with the intention of sightseeing and learning the language, but I ended up becoming an ambassador for a country that has been unfairly misjudged. I listen to stories of rich history as locals reminisce about their experiences. I empathize with those who have been isolated and suspected, solely based on a reputation associated with their citizenship. I feel for their limited choices and scarcity of opportunities. I sympathize for their undeserved complacency, born out of necessity to settle and not out of choice.

Yet, I feel a great respect and admiration for their resilience.

Colombia is by no means paradise. Like every other country, it has its faults, perhaps more than others, which the government is trying hard to correct. Remnants of their dark past abound in the form of statues and street art. Landmarks are visual representations of their tribulations and triumphs. Memories are etched and shared as a reminder of their journey but also as an inspiration for progress. Traditions and recipes are celebrated as a gleaming portrayal of their pride and patriotism.

Admittedly, I came to this country naively clinging to its stigma. But since I arrived, I have been humbled by my disproven judgments. For the time being, I have settled in this country and embraced its idiosyncrasies while taking part in its transition. I have yet to plan my next move, but one thing is certain: I intend to continue this lifestyle. Before, I patterned my life in accordance to societal standards and now it's time I abide by my own. Perhaps one day when I get tired of moving, I will settle down. Until that time, I will continue to scour the world for places to explore, people to meet, and realizations to discover.

As I write my story, I remember with vividness all my adventures, blunders, awkwardness, and mishaps. In contrast to the stories I have highlighted, I have also experienced heart-pounding, tear-inducing, and nerve-wracking situations. I have been detained. I have had my possessions stolen. I have witnessed brawls, quarrels, and crimes. I have had my share of doubts, fears, disappointments, and misfortunes. I have felt vulnerable, homesick, jaded, and disheartened.

Despite it all, I chose to focus on the aspects of my journey which have kindled a sense of childlike wonder within me. I pondered on wisdom, learning, and progress. I contemplated the impact of change, movement, and growth on my life. I focused on journeys, discoveries, and adventures. I embraced possibilities, vastness, and freedom.

I questioned, I leapt, and I soared.

I write to share my unfinished adventures, hoping to incite the same sense of enthusiastic wonder. Beyond limited beliefs awaits a world of infinite surprises.

Name: Debra Hall

Nationality: American

Country of Residence: United States

Why She Left the Rat Race: Debra was encouraged to stick with a large company, make a long-term commitment, and earn a pension. Over time, she realized the price was too high. "I was exhausted. I never saw my family, let alone any friends. I hadn't even noticed it along the way, but over time I had abandoned all my social circles. In the few minutes I had to myself each week, I just wanted to be left alone."

CHAPTER EIGHT
Freedom at Forty
Debra Hall, *United States*

I QUIT MY FULL-TIME JOB WITHOUT a plan. I had no idea what I was going to do next. I only knew that something had to give. I had been working full-time for as long as I could remember. Looking back, I'm not sure if I thought I *had* to work a full-time job, or if I was just comfortably stuck in that job. It had been so many years since I had been excited about something, anything, that the word "excitement" was no longer in my vocabulary. I was over forty years old when I finally left the 9-to-5 grind. Though I wish it had been sooner, I feel incredibly blessed to have escaped at all. In my parents' day, quitting a secure full-time job wasn't something that people did.

I grew up in an ordinary family. I lived in a modest home, had a father who worked, a stay-at-home mother, and two brothers. I was the middle child and the only girl.

My parents raised the three of us with the same values. We were taught that to succeed in life you have to get an education and find a good job. My parents were not so old-school to believe that, as a woman, I needed to find a husband, have kids, and stay home. Don't get me wrong—they wanted me to get married and have kids, but they were ok with my being a "modern" woman who worked. Modern woman sounds funny these days, but a lot has changed over the years. Growing up when I did, it was a very uncommon situation to find a home on my block, or even in my neighborhood, that did not include a stay-at-home mom.

In fact, as a young girl that was my plan: to have a family and raise children. This changed with age— both *my* age and the age in which I lived. The economy and world changed as I grew up. So did my focus. I found a love of numbers. Yes, numbers. Most of my friends hated math and business, but I would choose creating a spreadsheet over creative writing any day. By the end of high school, I knew I wanted to work, even if a Prince Charming came and whisked me off my feet. I had found my calling.

To my father, an acceptable job was one at a large international company that would offer a pension and stocks to secure your future. This was the norm when my parents were in the workforce. People would start out entry-level and grow from within the company ranks. Thirty or forty years later, they would retire.

"You have to work for a large corporation and get a pension. It's the only way." This was the mantra my father repeated often while my brothers and I were growing up. He still says it to this day.

I don't know if I will be financially comfortable one day, or ready for retirement in twenty years. . . . But I do know that I am determined to make a path for myself in this digital, virtual work environment and to never step foot inside an office again (unless it's for a client meeting).

My father worked as a big shot vice president for an international pharmaceutical company, traveling to other countries to negotiate drug sales and distributions with government officials. Though we didn't see him often, his career choice ensured we always had a roof over our heads, food on the table, and the necessities of a good life. Our house was the last in the neighborhood to get a VCR, a microwave, and even a cordless phone. I thought for a long time that we couldn't afford all the new toys and electronics. I know now that we could. My father was just incredibly frugal. I understand it today, but as a child or a teenager, I did not know we never had a mortgage and that college was paid in cash for all of us. My father is now retired and very comfortable.

I don't know if I will be financially comfortable one day, or ready for retirement in twenty years. Honestly, right now I am scared I will never be able to retire. But I do know that I am determined to make a path for myself in this digital, virtual work environment and to never step foot inside an office again (unless it's for a client meeting).

I am a 44-year-old woman, with a long-term boyfriend of 23 years and a son. I earned my college degree in accounting and went right to work for a small local contractor in Queens, New York. This

Unexpected Lifestyle Changes: Though not entirely unexpected, it was the time Debra was able to spend with her son before he left for college that mattered most to her. "I learned about his political views, his family views, and his thoughts on his peers and trends. They were things I wouldn't have spent much time worrying about, but they brought me so much closer to understanding this amazing person I had brought into the world. I am grateful I got to know him as a man."

may have been where I learned that I am a nester of sorts. I get comfortable and stay put.

I was with that firm for ten years, but after 9/11 we lost many of our clients, and business slowed down. It was time to change positions. Today, many young adults have worked at ten firms in less than ten years, always changing jobs and industries, searching for a better place or a better opportunity. I didn't understand the new generation. I always thought you were supposed to work hard and stay loyal. If you did that the company would reward you. It's what I was taught.

At this point, my brothers had finished their degrees and were working for large corporations and government agencies. They struggled and lived pay-check-to-paycheck. They always needed help from my parents to pay their rent or electric bill. My father insisted that my next position needed to be with a large, Fortune 500 type company. I was confused and mildly insulted. I am the only girl in the family, but I also never needed a handout. I worked hard like I was supposed to and budgeted frugally as I had watched my father do. I was able to buy a home and not rent like my brothers. But somehow, I still had it wrong.

Next, I found a position at a small firm. That was another four years of commitment on my part and being overlooked for advancement and raises on theirs. My boyfriend was working in sales at the time. I was not necessarily the breadwinner, but I had a secure salary that did not fluctuate as sales often can. After many talks with my boyfriend, we agreed it was time for me to search for a job in Manhattan. That is, after all, where the money is, and I longed for a position where I would be more appreciated and able to share my ideas.

I had always avoided going into the city for work because I feared the long commutes and long work hours. But since my son was about ten years old, I could go further from home and his school without worrying about him. I landed the first interview. It was at a small firm again, but in a niche area of IT and consulting. It appeared to offer promising opportunities for growth.

The first year was exciting. I was in Manhattan, dressing like a business person. There were no more sneakers and jeans in the office. By the second and third year I had made my little nest. I was comfortable. But the hours were much longer. I was out of the house at 6:30 am, home at 7:30 pm, and then I cooked dinner, did laundry, helped my son with homework, and found time for my 'husband' (boyfriend is a funny term after two decades). I thought I had it all under control. I had become the *Modern Woman*.

It took me longer than it should have to realize I

was giving away too many years of my life for too
low a paycheck. About two years ago it hit me that
the almost four-hours of commuting each day on
top of a 9-hour workday
was not the best scenario.

I was exhausted. I never
saw my family, let alone
any friends. I hadn't even
noticed it along the way,
but over time I had aban-
doned all my social

> **The Best Thing About
> Work Beyond Wages:**
> "There is no clock, no
> one asking me if I
> finished my project yet.
> There is just me being in
> charge of my time."

circles. In the few minutes I had to myself each
week, I just wanted to be left alone.

My exhaustion and the lack of interaction with my
family became an almost daily fight at home. My husband has always been my cheering squad. He tells me
all the time that I could be more, do more, and
should get paid more. He never believed I should be
a homemaker; he says I am too smart for that. But
now, all of a sudden, he insisted I quit my job. He
wanted dinner at dinnertime, not 9 pm at night. He
wanted time together. Our son misses you, he told
me. I miss you.

I was stubborn, confused, and exhausted. I was
not willing to quit my job for a man; women's
rights are hard-earned. But my son was missing
out on time with his mom. That is what really

hurt. I had missed so much without realizing it, mostly because my husband had handled everything while I worked.

As a salesman he was setting his own schedule. He managed all the doctor and dentist visits, drop-offs and pick-ups from school, cleaning the house (well, hired someone for that, but it still counts since I wasn't doing it). He managed all the sports and school functions too. I heard about my son's school issues secondhand, through his father:

> **Top Tip:**
> "Don't be discouraged by the time it takes to build a business. Finding clients is, in some ways, more challenging than the work itself. Keep at it and you will slowly find your niche and your clientele."

girl trouble, his views on life, and more. I had not witnessed the moments that had transformed him from a boy into the young man he had somehow become along the way. All the moments I could never get back with my son began to weigh on me, adding to the stress at home and work. I felt overwhelmed with guilt.

Even this did not change anything right away. I am a nester, and my father's voice still rang in my head. "You have to stay at a company and be loyal," that voice reminded me. "Then, when you retire, you will be rewarded."

Fast-forward two more years. That's two more years of being miserable. Two years of making my family miserable. My son was less than a year from starting college. He would be spending his final year with us visiting schools and working on applications. I had only a few months that I could be involved in his life before he went out into the world.

Finally, I decided it was time for a change. I wanted to set my own schedule, spend time with my son before he left, and eat dinner with my family at a socially perceived "normal" dinner time.

Like I said, I had no plan, no idea about what I was going to do. I went to the CEO's office and offered my resignation with a 6-week notice to hire and train my replacement. It was an amazing moment. I felt free. I was not worried about the company. All the stress seemed to vanish. I had no backup plan but for the first time—with no plan, no job prospect and nothing on the horizon but uncertainty—I was excited about something, anything, everything. It was as if having no direction empowered me.

I started counting down the days to when I would be officially unemployed. My husband wanted to know what I planned to do. My father was happy I was leaving a small firm, but at the same time insisted I needed to work for a giant company while I still had time to earn a full pension. With only enough savings to stay home for three or four months, I decided to take an online master's course through the end of the year. I could spend Thanksgiving and Christmas with my family, while also ensuring that my time off didn't raise any red flags on my resume.

My husband was satisfied. My father was satisfied. I was satisfied. I took a deep breath and began to enjoy my time away from work. I fully expected to find another job after a few months breathing room. Funnily enough, though, I liked being home. I liked doing laundry, cooking meals, and grocery shopping in the middle of the day when everybody else was at work. It is amazing how many errands you can get done on a weekday. I still got up early. I just went right to class and did homework. I stopped when I wanted, started again when I wanted. There was no clock, no one asking me if I finished my projects. There was just me, in charge of my time.

I had never worked at a company that offered remote work options for employees, but I had heard of it. If it can work like my online classes, I thought, my life could stay my own. I researched remote jobs and freelance options. I began to apply for anything that was work-from-home. The search was long and yielded few results. After six months at home, I had spent all my savings and still had no remote job offers or prospects.

On the plus side, I was finally spending time with my son. At first it was hard, like pulling teeth, to get any conversation going—he is, of course, a teenage boy. Pretty soon we found our groove: a 30-minute car ride from school each night let me get the recap on what was going on in his world. My *first* attempt to connect with him by rattling off non-stop questions over dinner had not been well-received. But the relaxed car ride, with nowhere for him to run, worked. After a few weeks he began to offer stories and highlights of his day without my asking. I learned about his political views, his family views, and his thoughts on his peers and trends. They were things I wouldn't have spent much time worrying about, but they brought me so much closer to understanding this amazing person I had brought into the world. I am grateful I got to know him as a man.

We were able to do college visit road trips on weekends. We worked together to narrow down school choices and options. I even learned that what I had believed would be his major was not at all what he planned to study. As a senior, homework was light so we had time after dinner to watch television together or go to a movie. The best activity for me was being able to go to museums. My husband doesn't like them, but my son does, and we would take turns picking which one to go to next.

I spent the better part of a year being able to travel, go to shows, or visit museum without having to worry about a stack of deadlines waiting at an office. I was hooked. I wanted to keep this lifestyle. I refocused on what I needed to be able to work from home. I had the technology, a quiet workspace, and years of experience. So, what I was doing wrong? After mulling it over, the answer materialized. I hadn't refocused my salary requirements. I began taking small projects, pretty much anything I could get. I found that I could get work, it just wasn't going to pay a New York City wage. The work at home environment, I came to realize, is global. Living in NYC freelancing online is hard when you are competing with people who can do the same job for a tenth of the fee I wanted to charge.

My husband had grown tired of me being home all the time, with the small odd jobs I worked that did not pay nearly enough to reach my accustomed salary. He asked me to talk to an acquaintance of his who had a company that needed a bookkeeper to straighten things out. I wasn't thrilled, as that meant going to an office, but I needed the money. We agreed I would work two half days a week, at my old salary rate per hour, to help them get on track. The assignment ended up opening doors. It allowed me the time I needed to pursue a fully remote work environment. Plus, compared to what I had been doing most of my life, working in an office only one day a week still felt like a vacation.

The hunt for clients continued, and slowly I began to see results. As I taught myself the ins and outs of working for myself, I learned a lot about *myself*. In many ways, searching for work is harder than the actual work. After a year of throwing darts on freelance websites and through job posts, I finally developed darts that stuck. I still help out that company two days a week, but I have found four other firms in similar situations that I can work with remotely. I have the flexibility to work whenever I want, so long as I meet deadlines. It is as though I have four part-time jobs. It keeps things interesting.

My contracts afford me the flexibility to live my life the way I see fit. When you work for yourself, the only schedule you adhere to is your own. Now that I have found my remote niche and long-term client work, my family has begun discussing where we should move for retirement. I have a job that I can take anywhere and have learned the skills I'll need to continue this lifestyle for years to come. It took time, but I finally have a career I love without the burden of a 9-to-5 office job.

☙❧

Name: Terry Gachanja

Nationality: Kenyan

Country of Residence: Kenya

Why She Left the Rat Race: Fired by an employer who didn't want to pay mandatory maternity leave, Terry found herself a young mother without work. With motherhood on the horizon, she decided to look forward instead of backward. "I decided not to apply for 9-to-5 jobs but instead to do something else from home so that I could be near my baby all the time."

CHAPTER NINE
Choosing Jayden
Terry Gachanja, *Kenya*

MY NAME IS TERRY GACHANJA AND I am many things. I am a mother, a Kenyan, a wife, and a daughter. I am also a freelancer.

In 2014, I decided to work from home. I didn't have a source of income and I badly needed one. I was desperate for a solution. One day, I Googled how to start a business from home. I found many results and began sifting through all the information. I learned about working online, which I never knew existed. It's like a veil was lifted off my eyes and I could see clearly. I wondered why I had not found out about this earlier but as the saying goes, God's timing is always best.

From this part of the world, working online is unheard of and not understood. How can you even explain it to someone? What does it even mean? People ask questions like: did your parents educate you so that you can work with the Internet? They say: you should have a white-collar job, an office job just like everyone else. Part of the incomprehension I received from those around me came from their disbelief. You cannot possibly make the same amount of money on the internet that you can in a regular office job, they told me.

These are some of the sentiments I used to get from my friends and family when I tried explaining to them that I was considering working online from

---

From this part of the world, working online is unheard of and not understood. How can you even explain it to someone? . . . You cannot possibly make the same amount of money on the internet that you can in a regular office job, they told me.

---

home. They didn't believe there was anything like that in the first place. Even I did not fully understand the idea. Remember, I had just seen from Google that it was possible to work online, but I still hadn't secured a job.

When I told my mother that I was considering not going to work anymore, and instead I would work from home, she snapped at me. She told me how I wasted the fees my father paid for my college. I tried reasoning with her, but she told me I needed to leave my baby with her and go back to work. What she did not know is that I had lost my job several months earlier, during the ninth month of my pregnancy. She thought I was on maternity leave.

I had started working a 9-to-5 job in the year 2010. I worked for three straight years with a wonderful marketing company. I loved my job since it involved a lot of traveling. I worked hard and there were never any complaints about my work. While working with this marketing company, I met my boyfriend who later became my husband. During that period, I conceived. I continued with work without any issues until I was seven months pregnant. Then, I noticed some problems with the company. My supervisor started having issues with my work, which he had never had before.

He would surprise me randomly while I was performing my duties and I felt there was more than met the eye. One time he came and told me that he had received a phone call that I might be selling some company products without their knowledge. It wasn't true, and so this really caught me off-guard.

While all this was happening, I was already eight months pregnant.

Little did I know, the company did not want to pay my maternity leave. They were looking for reasons to terminate my contract. All this I learned later from a colleague who was close to my supervisor. Just before I clocked my ninth month, I received a termination letter without any benefits at all. To make the matter worse, the company refused to pay my monthly salary for which I had already worked. I went home empty handed after working diligently in this company for about three years. This is not uncommon in Kenya. It was September 2013.

Unexpected Lifestyle Changes: Terry has been able to mentor other would-be freelancers in Kenya, opening their eyes to possibilities online. "Our formal economy can only be accessed by a select few," she writes, "but the online economy is open to all."

I thought of suing the company and even got a letter from a lawyer to do so. But I decided to let God avenge me since I knew I didn't deserve that kind of treatment. I went home and sank into depression. This was indeed a very trying moment for me because I needed money for my soon-to-arrive child.

In October of the same year, God blessed me with baby Jayden and I temporarily forgot my problems. I focused on what I already had at the moment. With the little savings I had, I finished my baby shopping and my fiancé helped with the other bills. Despite the fact that I was broke, I'd say I felt peaceful. Some kind of serenity came with welcoming Jayden to this world, but it would not last.

By December that year, my savings had run out and I had to rely fully on my fiancé for finances. We were not living together at that time and borrowing cash isn't fun, especially if you are used to having your own money. You have to account for every penny spent and you worry about repaying every dollar as the bills get higher.

I had to make something else work for me, but another problem arose. My baby boy was the kind that cries all the time. They are termed "high need babies." He is well fed, has a clean diaper, and is not sick, but he will still demand 24-hour attention from me. This was very draining and even if I found a job, just how was I going to work with this kind of a baby?

I decided not to apply for 9-to-5 jobs but instead to do something else from home so that I could be near my baby all the time. This was a difficult situation. By choosing not to get a new job in my career field, I worried I was compromising my career altogether. But a woman has to do what a woman has to do when faced with certain life challenges.

I decided to sacrifice my career and stay at home for the sake of my baby.

I felt guilty at times for not going back to working 9-to-5, especially because I was receiving numerous phone calls asking me to interview with various companies. I would attend some interviews and not others. At one time, I got an offer, but I weighed the options and decided not to take it. How could I leave my baby with my mother and go back to working 9-to-5? Was work that important compared to my own child?

It was then that I found freelancing. But getting started was a challenge. My mother demanded I leave the baby with her and return to work. My father refused to talk about the matter. Why did my society regard a 9-to-5 job so highly and disregard everything else? Why didn't anyone try to understand where I was coming from? Why didn't anyone try to put themselves in my shoes and at least empathize with me? I kept reading online about freelancing and learning more about what was possible.

In February 2014, when my baby was five months old, I came across a company called Odesk. Today it is called Upwork, an online job portal that connects freelancers with potential clients via contract job listings. It's from there that my freelance career was born. I found many online opportunities which I believed were a good fit for me. I applied to so many jobs, but initially I couldn't land anything. I faced competition, especially from other freelancers who were offering the same skills for much less. They could get hired and I couldn't. Language was also a barrier. Some clients from developed countries could see my potential, but they wanted to hire native English speakers most of the time.

The Best Thing About Work Beyond Wages: "I finally live life on my own terms and I work whenever I want to."

I pressed on. I kept applying and finally got my first job from an amazing American company. They accepted that I wasn't a native English speaker and hired me for a full two-year, part-time contract.

English is my fourth language so I had to learn a lot of English grammar to fit in my new role. My boss was an awesome person. She was very accommodating and corrected me with patience. Within a month or two, I had comfortably fit into my new freelancing role. I worked diligently for this American company until my contract ended in 2016.

I learned many things. Since the job was only part-time, I could apply for other small jobs online at the same time. I could do them alongside my main job. With that, I could make a living and make more money than most people who work in offices in Kenya. I could finally afford a lifestyle that I desired, but, most importantly, I was near my baby all day. Whenever I felt like seeing him, I could see him. I didn't have to ask for permission to go see my son since I was working from my home office.

Top Tip:
Terry advises people to hit the ground running, jumping in with both feet. "Utilize both free and paid courses to master a skill. Learn every day and do not lose hope when you fail."

Working online also came with challenges, especially when my first contract as a freelancer ended. I couldn't find a stable job like my first job. All I used to get was one-time projects, which I appreciated, but I needed something that enabled me to have money all the time.

That's when I graduated to other things, like blogging, on top of my freelancing career.

I learned how to set up blog posts, do keyword research, and rank my posts on Google for traffic. With my blog posts I could promote other people's products which is known as affiliate marketing.

This became my second source of income online. The commissions I received from my affiliate marketing was enough for me to get by, especially during those months when I couldn't land a free-lance job from Odesk.

I still blog but I do it part-time. Maybe once or twice a week. From blogging, I graduated to internet marketing.

I learned about email marketing, ecommerce, and CPA marketing (cost per action).

My world was getting bigger. I took some free and some paid online courses and perfected my skills. I saw how people were living the laptop lifestyle by using these kinds of online business models and I decided to dive in fully. I got into ecommerce and opened my first Shopify store. My store sold women's beauty products. I made so much money from this store that I was even able to build my father a house. This is when he first spoke about my decision to quit my 9-to-5. He saw that I had found a new way to make a living, and that it was working.

I sold beauty products through my Shopify store for the whole of 2016, and then I began selling other things, like crafts from Africa, using the same store, and many other things. I also ventured into Amazon and eBay. Things were finally coming together. I couldn't thank God more.

My biggest challenge was getting targeted cus-tomers, which is a craft I learned slowly. It took time and guidance from other people who were doing well in this career path. From ecommerce, which I still run with the help of other people, I learned CPA marketing. I made some good money with this business model and I still do.

I have been able to mentor people from my country who were struggling financially, especially those who could not land a job. The unemployment rate in Kenya is up to 60 percent. The corruption that is so rampant here has denied many skilled and educated people their chance to get better jobs. To get a job in this country, you have to know someone. If you don't then you are doomed. Our formal economy can only be accessed by a select few, but the online economy is open to all.

I have worked with over 1,000 young people so far, teaching them what I have learned and showing them the possibilities available for them to make money online. It's a way of giving back to society and of thanking God for enabling me to understand great and wonderful things that I knew nothing about.

I finally live life on my own terms and I work whenever I want to.

I have much to say to those who desire to work online and don't know where to begin. When you are fully committed to working online, jump in with both feet. Learn and learn and learn all you can, wherever you can. Utilize both free and paid courses to master a skill. Learn every day and do not lose hope when you fail. Never give up, press on, and always remember what you really want out of your online career.

Is it time with your child like I wanted? Is it a more flexible work schedule? Is it more money to pursue your life purpose? Whatever your reason is for wanting to work online, allow it to be the main motivator and a constant reminder of why you will never give up.

Remember, challenges and stumbling blocks are just distractions to make you lose your focus. Hang on and never lose your faith. Always believe in yourself and in your abilities.

Be blessed.

Name: Gayle Aggiss

Nationality: Australian

Country of Residence: N/A: Travels full-time

Why She Left the Rat Race: Struggling with debilitating anxiety, Gayle left the rat race to work on herself and find her own happiness in the world.

CHAPTER TEN
From Nursing to Abroad
Gayle Aggiss, *Australia*

ANXIETY. IT WAS A HELL THAT my own brain had created, a prison that I spent my days and nights in, and whose walls I somehow reinforced. Anxiety was a punishment for something terrible I'd never done. It was days of fear and isolation. One of the worst things about anxiety is that it cuts you off from the people who could help you, if you let them. Anxiety was nights of bad dreams and waking up in a sweat, convinced that I was dying.

I thought that I would die in that prison, and some days, I was worried that I would just continue *living* in it. It hadn't started out this way, but it's really easy to fall into a rut and become trapped there.

I was seventeen when I chose a career. Like most seventeen-year-olds, I was confused about everything. The fact that you are supposed to make huge, life-altering decisions as an upside-down teenager is one of the strangest realities of our culture. But I went along with it and I chose to go into nursing.

Why nursing? My mother had recently recovered from a nearly fatal bout of cancer and I had spent the last few years of my schooling looking after her. I had helped her move through chemo and watched

---

I was seventeen when I chose a career. Like most seventeen-year-olds, I was confused about everything. The fact that you are supposed to make huge, life-altering decisions as an upside-down teenager is one of the strangest realities of our culture.

---

her battle through the emotional fallout. I learned that I was good at caring for people, and that I had a strong stomach. With no other real idea about what I wanted to do, nursing seemed like a good choice. It wasn't.

I'm Australian. If there is one thing that you should know about Australians, it is that we travel. We love to travel. We revel in travel. We are perfectly situated to travel. With Asia nearby, it's easy to hop on a plane and go somewhere across the ocean for a week. Lots of people who grow up in Australia take short trips with their families during their teenage years. Bali is a great place to spend Schoolies, the week of partying that Australians partake in at the end of high school. For many Australians, travel to Asia is an introduction to overseas travel and often begins a life spent exploring different places.

I missed this initiation into the travel culture. I was worried about money and decided to be sensible. I signed up for my degree and began to prepare for my new life. But I soon discovered that I hated nursing. It was more than boring. I didn't like being surrounded by sick people, sad people, people who were at the end of their rope. Most of all, I didn't like being responsible for people's lives and health. I didn't like the idea that I might make a mistake that resulted in someone's death. It was too much for me to handle.

The one thing nursing did give me was a way to make money. Before I knew it, I was working as a caregiver in nursing homes. It seemed like a good way to make money in the healthcare world without the burden of literally holding someone's lifeline. I fed people, showered them, and got them changed. I kept them calm when their minds were determined to destroy them. I provided company to people who had outlived their friends and family. Many were completely alone in the world.

I also quit my nursing program. I hated it, didn't want to do it, and was afraid to do it. So why wouldn't I quit? The trouble is that I had no actual career to replace it with.

So, I drifted.

I moved from city to city, from nursing home to nursing home. I didn't travel outside of the country and I didn't study. Along the way, the shell that I wore around myself got smaller. I got smaller. I wasn't taking care of myself. I wasn't eating right, and I drank too much on the weekends. I was living like a student, but I was decidedly an adult.

The debilitating anxiety began when I had a health scare. I started to feel dizzy and lightheaded all the time. I had trouble concentrating. I constantly felt tired and faint. All these symptoms could be and were eventually fixed with better lifestyle choices and some time, but my brain went into full panic mode. That was it.

Anxiety. I had it and no matter what I did, I couldn't seem to let it go. Everything seemed to set it off. New places. Old places with new faces. Taking risks. Sleeping. Going outside

Anxiety robs you of so much. At the time, you think it protects you, but when you look back, all you can see are the things that you missed. The adventures, the good, bright memories that you're supposed to make at this time of your life are missing because you never had the chance to experience them. You were too busy being anxious. Every holiday and birthday is tainted by the anxiety, and it is impossible to make good memories when you're held in its grip.

My anxiety was made worse by another family crisis. My parents owned their own business and lived a few hours away from the city I was living in. While I struggled with anxiety, they went bankrupt. It was a slow process, drawn out over a year as they fought to keep something, anything. They failed. They lost everything. They lost their business. They lost their home. When it became clear that everything was lost, I went to stay with them so I could help pack up the house. We packed up everything they were allowed to keep. I stayed to support them while they started all over again in their forties. As you can imagine, this didn't help with the anxiety I was feeling. It amplified it.

> **Unexpected Lifestyle Changes:** Choosing a life of travel. Teaching overseas helped Gayle to come out of her shell and learn to enjoy her life. "It was the beginning of so much more life. It was the end of things as well. I'm not the same person who left Australia and my life two years ago."

Stubbornness was my savior. It was always the one thing I had going for me. My stubbornness is legendary, and it became the tool I needed when anxiety tried to rip apart my life. I used it well. I found my own way out.

I stubbornly sat on benches in crowded shopping centers with sunglasses on, so no one could see my eyes, and I let myself panic, over and over again, without letting myself leave. I'd sit there sweating, my legs so shaky that I don't think I could have walked even if I'd let myself leave. Anxiety wrung me out like a wet cloth and yet, despite the lies that my brain screamed at me anxiety didn't kill me.

> **The Best Thing About Work Beyond Wages:**
> For Gayle, the best thing about working as a contractor overseas is the ability to experience new places and cultures with every new contract. "There have been losses and there have been gains, but I wouldn't change my choice to teach overseas for anything. In fact, I'm spending a lot of my time at the moment planning where to live next, and that's almost as fun as actually being there."

Each day, I made myself sit on the bench longer, and longer, until I was certain that my heart was going to burst. After a few weeks of this, my body and my brain learned that the panic didn't mean bad things were going to happen, and my body let it go, just like that.

I learned to retrain my brain, forcing it onto a different, straighter track every time it began to spiral back on itself, refusing to let it continue the familiar, panicky circles. That's one of the worst things about anxiety, and it's also what causes the panic attacks and the terrible feelings. Your brain latches onto a pattern of thinking, a bad circular pattern, and goes around and around until it feels as if it's twisting inside your skull, ripping itself apart.

But patterns have to be learned. And new patterns are always possible.

Little by little, I learned the different techniques that worked for me. Slowly, I fought my own personal demons, again and again until they were too tired to attack back. I went back to work as soon as I could, which was just in time because I was running out of savings even while living with my parents. I moved out once they were more stable, ready to start my own life one more time.

Although I was still struggling with the tail-end of the fear, I began to make big changes in my life. One of the first things I did was enroll in an online university. I chose the online option because I still wasn't comfortable going into school every day.

Australia is big and spread out, and the online university system is pretty good. All the big universities have online courses and the degree you earn is exactly the same as the one you would earn if you actually went into the classroom. You listen to lectures, read book chapters online, and comment on the material on the subject forums. The forums are a great place to argue with other students, consider other points of view, and generally get most of the benefits you would enjoy if you earned your degree in person. The forums taught me to interact again—online where I felt safer—where there was a barrier that protected me. I learned to communicate and share in this safe environment, which prepared me to fully go back into the world.

This time, I chose a Bachelor of Arts degree, a much better fit for me than nursing had been. Once I started the classes, I realized again just how much I loved to learn. With the arts degree program, I could take science subjects, learn about English literature, and dip my toes into sociology. I discovered a deep and abiding passion for philosophy and reignited my love for ancient history. The subjects fascinated me, my lecturers praised me, and I got used to interacting with other students through the forums.

Then a friend invited me to visit him in Thailand. I still hadn't been overseas, a fact that I mourned in the quiet times when there was nothing else to occupy or distract my mind. I'd always wanted to travel, but between my gradually improving mental health and lack of money, I thought it was still out of reach. Then, my friend pointed out that he had an apartment, so I wouldn't have to pay for accommodation.

> **Top Tip:**
> "Face your fears and allow stubbornness to be your savior."

I went.

I can't describe that first trip, the first time going through customs. I was bouncing out of my skin with excitement and terror all at the same time. I could feel my heart pounding but I didn't know if it was fear or joy. I went through customs convinced that something would happen, that I would be stopped or arrested or that somehow this chance to travel would just slip away. I sat on the plane in a daze, watching cartoons and other silly shows.

I landed in Thailand and it was the best time of my life.

The noises, the smells, the people, the strange foods. Eating chili omelets for breakfast and buying iced chunks of fruit to take back to the apartment at the end of the day both amazed and terrified me. I explored temples and gaudy statues. I stood at the side of the road and wondered how I would ever navigate the mess of bikes and cars without getting hit. I walked through enormous, gleaming shopping centers that were larger than most of the cities back home, marveling at the goods and arguing over prices.

I sat in bars at night and watched girls with sad eyes offer themselves to men who had been baked bright red by the harsh sun. I watched them disappear and reappear to start all over again.

I got foot massages. I cried at a green cloaked cemetery by the river. I ate strange meats that I stopped trying to identify after the first couple of times. I watched singing men dressed as women slink their way across the stage and learned to just keep moving no matter how aggressively people tried to sell me stuff I didn't want.

I loved it. And I wanted more.

There's nothing like that first trip, getting a taste of different air. For some, that first trip is a quick treat that's better once it's over, something they do and then are so happy to come home from. For me, it became an obsession. I finally knew what I wanted to do with my life: I wanted to travel. And I wanted to do it for longer than the seven-week holidays that Australians get each year. So I looked into teaching overseas.

There's a lot of information online about this these days. Whatever you want to know, you can find. You can choose a country and look at job advertisements. You can look at reviews from different companies that might hire you and see what

---

The first thing I realized was that I needed to finish my degree. There are still certain places that will give you a job without a degree, but they're usually semi-illegal and will treat you poorly. . . . I also realized that it would be a good idea to get some teaching experience, maybe even a teaching certificate.

---

qualifications you'll need to get the job you want. The first thing I realized was that I needed to finish my degree. There are still certain places that will give you a job without a degree, but they're usually semi-illegal and will treat you poorly. I'm nothing if not thorough and organized.

I also realized that it would be a good idea to get some teaching experience, maybe even a teaching certificate. I'd never taught before, but I was well acquainted with the idea of stage fright. I didn't want to get all the way to another country and freeze once I was in front of a class. I earned my CELTA certificate, an expensive choice, but the best qualification you can have for teaching overseas. It required four weeks of teaching, assignments, and intensive classes that were exhausting. I started yelling at my cupboards by the third week.

I was in class for eight hours a day and had an hour-plus commute each morning and afternoon. At home, I had hours of homework and studying. I also started to teach that very first week. That meant I had to stand up in front of a bunch of strangers and pretend that I knew anything at all about the language I'd spoken since the beginning of my life.

Just in case you were wondering, I really didn't know anything about it at first.

I think this was the time when my anxiety finally died and was buried. It just couldn't stand up to that kind of assault. My days were productive and peaceful. I passed the course, finished my degree, and got ready to leave.

My first teaching assignment was five months in Vietnam. I thought a shorter contract would be a good idea, just in case I didn't like it. I also decided to take an internship instead of going out on my own because I wanted some extra support for my first time teaching. Looking back, the internship was a mistake. Despite the extra support, the internship paid less, and life in Vietnam was expensive. We were teaching in public schools with about seventy students per class, and the pay wasn't even close to what I could have earned on my own. I wish I had been braver and started out teaching my own class, but any issues with my job were overshadowed by my new life.

Vietnam was fascinating. A group of us stayed in one big house with separate rooms and a shared kitchen and bathroom. It was in a local neighborhood, so there was nothing but small local stalls nearby to buy food from. No one spoke English and all the food was local. I learned to order in Vietnamese or with hand gestures and to ignore the waitress killing animals right in front of me after I ordered.

Living in Vietnam wasn't all good—I learned that being on the back of a motorcycle is the most terrifying thing in the world—but it was all worthwhile. I left with hundreds of vivid memories. I learned about a new culture, and about myself. By the time the internship finished, I knew I had made the right choice. I went home to Australia for a little while to visit family, then soon left for China. I taught there for a year and loved it.

When people ask me what it's like to live in China I never know what to say because the truth is, it was just life. It was getting up in the morning and trying to figure out how to use the washing machine when the only instructions were written in Chinese script. It was finding a place to buy my morning cup of tea, working out how to ask for it, and discovering a new tea that I still miss to this day. It was learning that I'm too tall to buy women's clothes, and that my feet are too big and too wide to fit in Chinese shoes. It was rats and firecrackers outside my window at five in the morning. It was teaching during the week and being able to jump on a plane for an hour to travel to other parts of Asia on weekends and holidays. It was walking a lot and finding restaurants with pictures and never quite fully grasping the language. It was getting sick and enjoying a faster internet than I had in Australia.

It was life, just in another country.

It was one of the best years of my life, and it was the beginning of so much more life. It was the end of things as well. I'm not the same person who left Australia two years ago. Many of the people I was friends with before I left aren't really a part of my life anymore. I didn't realize how much I had changed until I got back and saw these changes through other people's eyes. I saw that I don't fit in anymore with some people, and that's okay. That's life and it shows I have grown. On the other hand, some of my relationships are stronger than they've ever been.

There have been losses and there have been gains, but I would never change my decision to teach overseas. In fact, I'm spending a lot of my time at the moment planning where to live next, and that's almost as fun as actually being there.

Name: Ayelen Lamas

Nationality: Argentinian

Country of Residence: Argentina

Why She Left the Rat Race: After several years working as an illustrator, Ayelen's work started to become dull. She also began to worry about job security as there are very few jobs for illustrators in Argentina. She wanted more variety and job security. Her own client list could offer these things.

CHAPTER ELEVEN
Choosing Art
Ayelen Lamas, *Argentina*

I PUT DOWN MY STYLUS AND take a deep breath. Almost done, but I cannot relax yet: I must upload the files to the company server. Zero percent. Internet connections, or lack thereof, have failed me in the past. 15 percent. But it cannot today. 35 percent. The deadline is today. 55 percent. After four days of working overtime, all the muscles in my hand ache. 75 percent. My eyes are strained. My daily routine has been twelve to fourteen hours in front of a monitor. . . . But I still cannot blink, I must see this to the end. 95 percent. Almost there. In the last 5 percent, I suddenly become aware of all the danger that has been lurking: power outages, problems with the ISP, the laptop battery dying, or the cat yanking out the modem cable . . . 100 percent. I close my eyes and sigh with great relief. No matter how exhausted I feel, I would do it all over again. I love my job!

Let me introduce myself. My name is Ayelen. I live in Argentina. I am twenty-nine years old and have spent the last five years working as a freelance illustrator and designer. Each year, the projects have

---

I have been drawing for as long as I can remember. When I was five, my teacher was amazed at my use of perspective. At the age of ten, I could not wait for the school day to end so I could work on my "active projects."

---

become more important. I have worked with big names in the industry and I have won awards for my work. It was not easy then and it is still not easy . . . but it is one of the most gratifying parts of my life.

I have been drawing for as long as I can remember. When I was five, my teacher was amazed at my use of perspective. At the age of ten, I could not wait for the school day to end so I could work on my "active projects." By twelve, I had created several comics and I decided to start working on my coloring skills. I would stay up until the break of dawn to finish experimenting with water coloring. I was not going to "leave it for later." When I was seventeen, I started working on my own birthday gift. It took about five months to complete and included all the characters I had designed and drawn so far. That same year I finished high school. In 2006, I began attending graphic design classes at university and helped my mother at a buffet she ran at a school. I was not remotely interested in my first 9-to-5 job.

After a year at a job I hated, I saw an ad in the newspaper. A creative agency was looking for a colorist to work on comics and other projects. I wrote them but did not receive a reply. I wrote again. And again. I am not sure how many times I wrote to the agency, but eventually I got an answer. They said they liked my work, and although it needed improvement, I was hired! From 2009 to 2013, I worked as an illustrator and colorist from 8 am to 5pm, Mondays through Fridays, five days a week. I got one hour for lunch and two weeks of vacation every year. At first the work was trying, but I learned quickly and was very disciplined. It was not long until they put me in charge of the coloring team.

Fast forward another year. The work I once loved was becoming rather dull. I was not finding new challenges and I wasn't learning anything new. The agency worked with the same clients who often requested the same materials. I felt stalled and I hated it.

It was then that I decided to start taking on clients as a freelancer, to "rekindle the flame" as a colorist and illustrator. Although I was not directly involved in the process, I had seen my bosses negotiating fees and dealing with clients on countless occasions. I paid attention and learned a thing or two about the business end of the industry. This allowed me to ease into the process of finding clients, negotiating fees, managing a large schedule and making the deadlines. I was glad I did. When I took to the internet, I found my own clients with requests that were, if nothing else, new and different compared with what I had been working on previously. This was a challenge I gladly tackled.

Unexpected Lifestyle Changes: Stability has been the lifestyle change that Ayalen most appreciated. "As a freelancer, I know how to market myself and how to find work wherever I am. I provide a more solid and less fictitious stability than anyone else can offer me."

At first, freelancing was an "on-the-side" thing. The agency sustained my livelihood. After nine-hour work days and classes I did not have much time to devote to my freelancer clients, but I made myself do so. Even if I had had more time, I did not have enough clients to compete with the pay that I earned from the agency. Still, the few clients I had from freelancing allowed me to save enough money for a little vacation on the coast.

To be completely honest, apart from the challenge of new work pulling me away from a 9-to-5 job, I had already started considering that my position at the company was somewhat unstable. My ability to work in my chosen field was dependent on this agency. Being aware of this made creating and growing a client list a very interesting prospect. If the agency closed, how was I going to continue to make a living doing what made me happy?

My concerns were well founded.

Six months after I began taking on clients, the agency closed due to friction between the founders. In my country, when a company suddenly closes, employees are compensated with a sum of money proportional to their years of employment (and other variables). As I said, the few clients I had so far, were not enough to make a living, and the industry is severely underdeveloped here (finding that ad a few years back had already been incredibly lucky).

There was little to no chance of landing another job like that.

Before me stood a choice, or at least that would seem to be the case to the outside observer. I could freelance, or I could find a job outside of what I wanted to do. For me, there was no alternative. If I did not take the freelance road, it was very unlikely that I would have been able to continue doing what I enjoyed doing for a living. I decided to take the money from my compensation package and use it to buy some of the equipment I used in the agency and sustain myself until I had enough clients to make a living. The four months that followed were scary and full of anxiety. I was constantly questioning myself. Is this the right move? Will I succeed? There were too many questions to list. Routine offered a certain kind of respite. That peace of mind had flown out the window, but I had to hold on to the knowledge that I was doing my very best. I was scared, but I was not going to go through life without trying to bring my dreams to fruition. I owed this much to myself.

And then, one month, the numbers added up. I had made enough money to sustain myself without impacting my lifestyle or quality of living. Four months after my stable, 9-to-5 job had ended, I could proudly say that I made my living as a freelance illustrator. Few things in life are as sweet as the first time you say those words out loud to someone.

It was not an "every month is better than the last" kind of deal. The trick to being able to sustain my business year-round consisted in saving money during the good months so I could cope during months that were slow. For me, work is seasonal. I had slow seasons during Christmas and summer recess, and I had to save during the rest of the year knowing that there was not going to be the same amount of work during these times.

I planned ahead, took trips, attended workshops and conferences, or sometimes just rested, knowing that my free time would soon to be replaced with deadlines.

The Best Thing About Work Beyond Wages: "The opportunity to keep learning new things perhaps highlights the most exhilarating and priceless perk of freelancing: the ability to constantly challenge myself and never become bored by mechanical chores assigned by someone else. Freelancing gives me the reins to make myself a better me and enjoy the whole journey."

It was time to spread my wings, rather literally. It was 2014, and one year had passed since I started living as a freelance illustrator. I had never been on an airplane before then. My mom always wanted to see Easter Island, so I took her there. It was one of the most beautiful places I had ever seen. I felt newly blessed to be a freelancer. You don't fully appreciate it until you realize you can hop on a plane and go see the world on your own schedule. In a 9-to-5, you are only allowed to dream after office hours.

Top Tips:
"Freelancing requires great discipline. Deadlines have to be met if you want to make a serious living, a good living, as a free-lancer. It is hard work, but if you are diligent it allows you to sleep in and work most of your time in your pajamas."

During that first year and a half, I continued working with one of my former bosses while I selected the best web agencies to work with. This eventually led to more and clients and better paying work. In the end I found myself working mainly with two agencies.

The first agency offered many clients but the projects were smaller than what I was used to. It allowed me to see a whole new range of colors—so to speak. Each client requested a different style and theme. No two clients were the same. It was a tour de force. It allowed me to discover new styles and ideas. In the end it was not only a great learning experience, it was a paid one.

The other agency I worked with offered a smaller volume of projects, but they were larger and involved returning clients. It allowed me to meet some of the greatest and nicest people I have worked with to date, and to create a loyal client base. I worked with clients that taught me about all sorts of cultural backgrounds—I learned how to make Turkish coffee, and sashimi salad. I was also able to consistently return with larger projects that lasted several months and paid accordingly. This offered something that it is often thought of as lacking in my line of work: stability.

Stability is a funny thing. In hindsight, I now know that stability is best provided by yourself. Assuming stability is something somebody else, be it a small company or a big one, can offer you is a mistake. My 9-to-5 once closed their doors for a whole month, without warning. The livelihoods of my colleagues and I closed with those doors. The same thing happened, only more permanently, when the company shut down for good.

As a freelancer, I know how to market myself and how to find work wherever I am. I provide a more solid and less fictitious stability than anyone else can offer me.

My business did not stop growing. In 2016, I built my own website, drew in even more clients, and suddenly found that my work was no longer seasonal. Every season became high season. The trend continued and in 2017 I was awarded the "PromaxBDA Global Excellence Award 2017" for my work with the Disney Channel Latino's Halloween "Monstubre" campaign.

I had effectively elevated my game. It is not a moment you can put your finger on, but when you look back, you know it happened, and it is a great feeling. I had arrived. It had been a long road, but the perks of freelancing are worth all of the hard work. In addition to self-made stability, I had a variety of projects and sense of freedom. These are hard, if not impossible, to find in more traditional forms of employment.

I have worked on company logos and branding, children books, comics for teenagers and adults, corporate communications material, whiteboard videos, instructional comics, assets for video games, corporate training video games, and the odd client that requested something mature-rated. I have loved every minute of it for the variety alone. I am also finding that the more I grow in my career, the more often I can pick and choose the projects that interest me.

Another amazing perk of this line of works has to do with time. You are, for better or for worse, the absolute master of your time. Freelancing requires great discipline. Deadlines have to be met if you want to make a serious living as a freelancer. It is hard work, but if you are diligent it allows you to sleep in and work most of your time in your pajamas. Freelancing allows you to take a sudden and unplanned three-hour break to go meet a friend, watch a movie, or get a latte. I have also been able to pursue other interests and commercial enterprises, with an ease that traditional office hours would not allow.

In December 2017, for example, two freelancers and I worked together to form "Avanti Producciones." The three of us pooled together all our knowledge and experience to offer clients a broad range of options in the audio-visual media field. I am totally thrilled by this new adventure. I already see reflections of my own journey in this young but thriving agency. It requires me to limit the rate at which I take on new clients and projects, but I cannot escape the allure of the challenge. I am also seeing a lot of potential for learning new things, in new fields.

The opportunity to keep learning new things perhaps highlights the most exhilarating and priceless perk of freelancing: the ability to constantly challenge myself and never become bored by mechanical chores assigned by someone else. Freelancing gives me the reins to make myself a better me and enjoy the entire journey.

Name: Alison Wood

Nationality: British

Country of Residence: United Kingdom

Why She Left the Rat Race: When Alison started tallying how much time she spent in a place she didn't want to be, she knew something had to change. "Our lives are so precious to us and yet we waste them . . . As I thought about those seconds, minutes, hours and days spent sitting somewhere I really didn't want to be, I knew I couldn't waste any more time."

CHAPTER TWELVE
Stepping, Starting, Teaching
Alison Wood, *United Kingdom*

I AM A PERSON WHO PLAYS it safe. Even as a little girl I was always the responsible one, the one who took care of others. I was the eight-year-old, pushing thirty-five, who made sure Mum took her medication on time and who always, always wanted to do things properly.

Not, you would think, the background of someone who would throw everything up into the air, escape the shackles of corporate life and start living life on their own terms. Was it as easy as I made it sound just there? Not in the slightest. Was it worth feeling fearful at times? You bet it was. Is it still a work in progress? Most definitely.

Here's a little about my journey from safety to a new venture and how adventure can be whatever it means to you.

Little Girl Shy

I WAS BORN IN SURREY BUT during my childhood my parents moved around frequently, so we were never in one place for very long. My dad worked in the Stock Exchange in London when I was very small and we had a very stable life. However, when I was six my parents decided to go into business for themselves and purchased a shop in Kent. This shop sold a heady mix of shoes and toys—a strange combination, I know.

Upstairs, the shop was all formal as the local ladies came in for shoe fittings and chatted about the news of the town. Downstairs was a different story. It was a veritable wonderland for a child of my age. It was packed to the rafters with every type of toy you could imagine. This was the late 1970s— think space hoppers, dolls, teddy bears, movie merchandise, yes the *Force Was With Us*, and, of course, there were bikes and skateboards. Every day after school, and most weekends, I would spend time in the shop, listening to the conversations of the surrounding adults, dreaming of that next doll I wanted. I spent the vast majority of my time in my own head.

Toy heaven wasn't to last forever. When I was eleven, my parents decided to move to Devon and while my dad remained self-employed, it was always a bit of a tenuous existence going forward. Yes, we got by, but with very little to spare and there was always an underlying fear about not having enough money.

We also moved houses every 12 to 18 months. I think my parents always thought that the next house would bring us stability and happiness and while it did for a while, it was never quite enough. The "For Sale" sign would always go up again. I think that is part of the reason why safety was so

---

I stuck with the same job and lived in the same place for years, even though I knew it wasn't what I really wanted. I was too scared to go on a quest of my own.

---

important to me as an adult. I stuck with the same job and lived in the same place for years, even though I knew it wasn't what I really wanted. I was too scared to go on a quest of my own.

My childhood was a very happy one, but it was also a little unsteady, not only because of the moves but because my mum suffered from a serious heart condition and depression. This meant that, as an only child, I took on a lot of responsibility early on in my life. I would listen to my mum's worries and be very watchful that she was ok. This wasn't anyone's fault; it was just the way it was. It did mean, though, that my own feelings often got squashed down.

If anyone asked me how I was I would always say
"I'm fine" with a big smile on my face. Most of the
time I was fine, though I was also very shy.
Confidence was what all the teachers said I
needed—confidence in myself. "Imagine a big
syringe injecting you with confidence," someone
once told me at secondary school. They were trying
to help I'm sure, but I never did like needles. That's
not to say I didn't have fun as a child. I laughed
until I couldn't breathe most days, I danced on the
stage at the local ballet school, and I cartwheeled
until the sky became a turquoise blur. These activities, though, all happened within the confines of
my safety zone. They all took place at home, with
my family or with a small group of friends.

Speaking up in class or being the center of attention were definitely not things I enjoyed. I loved
school, but I didn't like to be singled out. Luckily, in
those days all the exams were written rather than
any form of project work. I just kept my head down
and managed to scrape the results I needed.

Stepping into the World

STEPPING OUT INTO THE WORLD OF university
was a huge deal for me. I was off to study English
Literature and History. While I was excited about
all the possibilities opening up before me, I was also

extremely scared. When I arrived at the Halls of Residence, which were to be my home for the next three years, it was like the ground had dropped away from beneath me. I literally couldn't eat for three days, an alien concept to a girl who can count chocolate as among her first words.

Slowly and safely, I began to build a business in my spare time. I learned the skills I needed to create websites, to market, to write successfully. I felt alive doing these things and the funny thing is that all the traits in myself that I had always looked down on—reliability, patience, empathy—became strengths in this new career of mine.

I overcame those early nerves and made friends, but I never really made the most of all the opportunities that college offered. I think, to be honest, I was pretty boring. I was so afraid of making a mistake that I really shied away from trying anything new. Inside, I felt like a person who was ready to take on the world, but the outside reflected something very different.

I settled in. I got my degree, my first job, a relationship, and a life.

It was a very safe life though, the same job for sixteen years working as an HR Manager. I rarely traveled, I never did anything unexpected, and I stayed in my comfort zone. I felt like if I just behaved, if I played by the rules, if I did my best, then surely things would go okay for me in life. They had to, right? I was working towards some distant, safe outcome. What the outcome was I had no idea, but keeping my head down was the only route I knew.

Reality Hits

IN 2008, I LOST MY MUM after a long period of illness. Six months later, I lost my dad, who suffered from dementia for the last years of his life. This was a huge wake-up call to me. What was the point of playing it safe all the time if you didn't know what was around the corner?

I didn't have any children, and I didn't enjoy corporate life. I knew I wanted something else. I knew I wanted to write and teach others. I wanted to break free from the constraints of sitting in endless meetings at work and constantly feeling like I was worth less than everyone else.

Slowly and safely, I began to build a business in my spare time. I learned the skills I needed to create websites, to market, to write successfully. I felt alive doing these things and the funny thing is that all the traits in myself that I had always looked down on—reliability, patience, empathy—became strengths in this new career of mine.

Breaking Free

I COULD HAVE GONE ON LIKE that for a long time, corporate life all day, working all evening and weekends on my business, and in fact, I did. I did that for nearly three years, and then

> **Unexpected Lifestyle Changes:**
> "All the traits in myself that I had always looked down on—reliability, patience, empathy—they actually became strengths in this new career of mine."

came the moment when everything changed. If you are expecting something dramatic, you are going to be sorely disappointed—this is me we are talking about, after all.

I was sitting at my desk at work one day, not really wanting to be there. The same daily thoughts of discontent were running through my head when I began thinking about time. Time ticking away that can never be brought back. Our lives are so precious to us and yet we waste them sometimes in the most mundane of ways. As I thought about those seconds, minutes, hours, and days spent sitting somewhere I really didn't want to be, I knew I couldn't waste any more time.

My business might not work out. I may not succeed. Fine. What was the alternative? Sitting at that
desk for another ten or twenty years? Reaching
retirement age, never having taken another single
step towards what I really wanted? I typed up my
resignation letter and I handed it in. I took the step.

After all the years I clung to safety it really was as
quick a decision as that. I am normally a person
who has to agonize over every step I take on the
path of life, but this felt
different. I was forty-
three at the time and the
pain of still sitting in that
desk at sixty-three was
something I simply
couldn't live with. The
cautious me will tell you that the decision was made
easier by the fact that I had already saved enough
money to keep me afloat for a year, and that you
might want to consider something similar if you are
thinking of taking the same step.

**The Best Thing About
Work Beyond Wages:**
"I haven't heard the
clock ticking for well
over five years."

Ultimately, that decision was the best I have
made to date. (I'm betting there are even better
ones ahead!) I felt free, and I felt confident. Was it
all going to be smooth sailing? Of course not,
nothing is. But it was so much better than the
alternative.

My New Adventure

So, what did this new adventure of mine look like? Basically, I took all the things I loved to do, all the things I was good at, and all the things I had learned along the way and I used them to help other people.

I set up my website AlisonMWood.com, and I offered website building tools and social media services. I then expanded my site's offerings to teach others what they needed to know to market and grow their own businesses. I loved this aspect of my business. As time has gone by, I have focused on writing and teaching. I have homed in on not just the practical side of running a business, but also about the most important aspect of all: mindset.

From someone who really struggled, and still does sometimes, to believe in themselves, this might seem a complete 180-degree pivot. However, because I have had all those fears myself about whether I am good enough to succeed, I can talk to people about the steps I took to overcome self-doubt and shyness. As a child, my fears outweighed my willingness to grow. As an adult I have worked to move past this, prioritizing growth and overcoming my fear.

How then did I go from little girl shy to wanting to teach others?

I started slowly. At first, I wrote down everything I was teaching. Then I did voice-over videos and, finally, I decided to throw live webinars into the mix. This is what scared me the most. You can't stop and press pause or re-record on a webinar. If you make a mistake you just have to keep moving forward, delivering the information people have signed up to receive.

I was absolutely terrified during my first webinar. I was shaking, worried that either the technology or my own ability to speak would let me down. The first thing I did during that first webinar was admit that I was terrified. After that, my worries seem to just fall away. I made mistakes and stumbled over things, but I kept progressing and improving. I love this form of communication now. In the beginning, I used to script out what I was I going to say, but now I just have slides that I use as prompts and I speak freely.

When I think back to how shy I used to be, it's hard to believe that me speaking on a webinar is even possible. Now I realize that when I was younger, I was always trying to fit into something someone else wanted of me. When I was younger, I was forced to speak in class, then later as an adult I had to speak in meetings, but these webinars were my own choice. I had taken back control of when and where and what I would speak about.

Mine isn't a big story of bravely traveling the world or taking daring strides to change something external. I know that it's a very small story of changing myself to allow room for more happiness and creativity into my life, but I think this is the story of many people's lives. It is universal. It can belong to everyone. My message now is to encourage everyone to pursue those things that bring them joy, whether it's starting a business, writing a book, painting a sunset, or volunteering for a cause they are passionate about.

> **Top Tips:**
> Realize that the confidence you need to succeed in business is exactly the confidence you will build by getting started. You don't need to throw all reason to the wind, you only need to take the first steps and watch your new life slowly unfold.

What I've Learned Along the Way

STARTING MY BUSINESS HAS BEEN AN amazing journey and I couldn't possibly explain here all that I have learned, both practically and emotionally—it would simply take too long. However, I do want to highlight a few of the key areas that will help anyone regardless of the type of adventure they want to take.

1. *Confidence*

   All my life, I believed that I needed to build more confidence before I went ahead and did something. The truth was actually the reverse of that. I needed to take action first, and then through that action my confidence would grow. We all have fears. Trying to pretend we don't or trying to hide from them can be more exhausting than facing them head on. I wish I had discovered that earlier in life, but better late than never.

2. *Mindset*

   Mindset is the biggest factor in whether you succeed or fail at anything. Spending time working on your mindset is never time wasted. It's vital to look to the future positively and with the belief that you are going to prevail. Yes, you might make mistakes along the way. Don't let these stop you. Learn the lesson from these mistakes and move on.

3. *Emotions*

   While being positive about the future is vital, you are going to experience a range of emotions as you move forward. It's important to acknowledge these and allow yourself to express fear, doubt, anger, joy, happiness, and everything in-between. You don't have to turn into an automaton who only expresses positivity. Allow yourself to be fully you.

4. *Support*

It's important to have support on your journey. If you can't find that in those closest to you, then look further afield. Make new friends, connect with people on social media, or join groups related to your quest.

5. *Consistency*

If you want to learn a new skill, market your business, or overcome a fear, consistency will make sure you stay the course. The key is to be so excited about the outcome that it becomes easy to keep taking daily steps.

If there's anything you have ever wanted to do in life, whether it's a new career, setting up a business, asking someone out, traveling, painting, then try it. Take that first step. You may step forward cautiously at first, maybe running your business alongside a traditional job, or traveling to the nearest big city before you plan your trek around the world, but take that first step nonetheless.

If you are like me, you might even find that some of the things that you don't like about yourself are in fact strengths. They just needed to be utilized in the right way. It has been well over five years ago since I left my corporate job behind. I have grown in ways I could never have imagined. It's been very tough sometimes, but I've always been focused on a purpose and something that I love. I haven't heard the clock ticking for well over five years.

I've also realized that being a person who plays it safe is actually okay. "It takes all kinds of people to make a world" as my Nan used to say. Embrace the person you are and allow others to be who they are.

The Future

FOR YEARS, IT SEEMED THAT I didn't really have any clear plan. I just ambled along and let life lead me, instead of me directing the course of my life. By stepping out of my safety zone I have changed that. Now I have so many hopes and dreams, so many goals for the future. If I want something now, I know that I have to hold the vision in my mind while taking practical steps towards getting it.

My main aim is to grow my business, but I am also writing my first fiction book, something that I have wanted to do for many years but never actually did any work on. Above all, what I have learned in the past ten years since the death of my parents, is that life is so, so short. We all spend too much time worrying about really tiny things that in the scheme of life, don't matter at all. No one looks back on their life and thinks about any of those inconsequential matters. We look back at the chances we missed and the things we achieved. We dwell on who we loved and what differences we made in the world.

Standing here at the midpoint of my life, I know that I am going to make the most of every second available to me. Whether you are just starting out on life's journey or whether you are further along than me, remember it's never too early and it's never too late to go after your dreams. The important thing is to be living your joy every day.

Name: Samar Owais

Nationality: Pakistani

Country of Residence: United Arab Emirates

Why She Left the Rat Race: Office politics, gender discrimination, and a culture of corporate public humiliation led Samar to leave the traditional workforce.

CHAPTER THIRTEEN
Building a Successful Freelance Business
Samar Owais, *United Arab Emirates*

SIX MONTHS. THAT'S HOW LONG I lasted in my first and to date my only full-time job.

I'd been headhunted for an eCommerce startup to become their Community Manager. The pay and perks were great. They were UAE's fastest growing startup and were fast gaining cult status because of their excellent service. Becoming their Community Manager would make me the face of their company—the person customers interacted with. It was a big responsibility but also a ton of fun. Who doesn't want to become a pseudo-celebrity in a small city like Dubai?

I diligently did my research before I joined. I met the team I'd be working with, talked to the Community Manager I'd be replacing, and had a long meeting with their HR Manager about growth opportunities and advancements.

It was great . . . at first. The job was everything I'd dreamed about. A fast-paced environment where ideas were implemented in a matter of hours. Crises were handled as they came in and customer feedback was taken seriously.

The team I was working with was the best. We watched out for each other and pitched in when things grew hectic.

The team I was working with was the best. We watched out for each other and pitched in when things grew hectic. But there was one thing I didn't factor in. Office politics. Boy did I suck at handling it! Not only did I not realize what was happening at first but when I did, I couldn't figure out how to deal with it. I was mansplained and talked over. My ideas were "bropriated." But the nail in the coffin was when I saw an employee being fired—publicly.

But there was one thing I didn't factor in.

Office politics.

Boy did I suck at handling it! Not only did I not realize what was happening at first but when I did, I couldn't figure out how to deal with it. I was mansplained and talked over. My ideas were "bropriated." But the nail in the coffin was when I saw an employee being fired—publicly.

Not only did the situation not warrant it, it was humiliating and demoralizing for the entire team. I began planning my exit strategy the same day.

The One Smart Thing I Did Before Quitting My Full-Time Job

AS SOON AS I REALIZED HOW high the startup's employee turnover rate was and how unpredictable, public, and humiliating their firing practices were, I started to think about resigning. Luckily, I'd been freelancing before joining the startup. I knew I didn't want another full-time job so going back to my freelancing roots was the best option.

But this time, I decided to take it seriously.

I took advantage of my great salary and enrolled in a writing course taught by James Chartrand of Men with Pens. The course was a turning point in my career. Not only did James make me a better writer, but her advice helped me treat my freelancing like a business and be treated as a business partner by my clients instead of an employee.

Discovering My Identity Issues and the Start of My Impostor Syndrome

AS SOON AS I QUIT, I started looking for freelance work. It wasn't long before my cold pitching led me to my first prospective client. Before they hired me, they said they wanted to have a video chat as part of their hiring process.

I balked.

I'm a head-scarf wearing Muslim from Pakistan. Baby, I had issues! Here's the surprising part though: I was caught off guard by this insecurity. I'd never felt this way before. Until recently, I'd been the public face of a company—you'd think this would be the least of my worries. But the UAE is a Muslim country. Women in hijab and expats from Pakistan are the norm here. The clients and publications I was targeting weren't used to someone like me.

So, the first time a prospective client suggested a Skype call, I hesitated. This hesitation cost me the client.

Every time I'd catch the attention of a high-paying client, I'd mess it up at the meeting stage. I just didn't want to do them. My insecurities started with being a Pakistani and a hijabi (headscarf wearer) and went all the way down to English being my second language.

I'd wake up every day thinking "Why the hell am I calling myself a writer in a language that is not my mother tongue?"

The few times I sucked it up and said yes to calls, I had to field well-meaning but condescending questions about my English (But you're from Pakistan. How is your English so good?) and my headscarf (Do you wear it in the loo too?).

The more questions I fielded, the more I hated these calls. Eventually, I stopped doing them altogether and decided I'd be an email-only business. I got quite adept at it too. I touted time zone differences and Skype being blocked in UAE as an excuse.

It worked. But I also gave up going after bigger clients because nobody wants to give $1,250 to a long-form blogger that they can't talk strategy with face-to-face.

Unexpected Lifestyle Changes: Though her original goal was to become a better writer and successful freelancer, Samar has become a confident business owner. She has cultivated a growth mindset and that has made all the difference.

Coming to Terms with My Identity as a Hijab-Wearing Pakistani Freelancer

IT TOOK ME A LONG WHILE to come to terms with who I was.

You don't get to choose where you're born. Sounds simple right? I have no business feeling ashamed of a country I spent some of my best years in. Yes, living in Pakistan can be the pits. It has a high crime rate and can resemble a war zone, but hey, plenty of people live, survive, and even thrive in war zones.

I'm quite proud of the skills living in Pakistan has taught me.

> **The Best Thing About Work Beyond Wages:** "I am always a partner, never an employee. I am the boss."

I learned how not to get caught in a crossfire and what to do in case you do. Every time I enter a room, I subconsciously note all of the exits and map out an exit route in case of an emergency.

Granted, it's not something that comes in handy when you're living in a peaceful country like UAE, but there are monsters everywhere. And I like knowing that I can think on my feet when my life is in danger.

As for the hijab—it's a personal choice. I wouldn't be caught dead outside without a headscarf just as millions of women the world over wouldn't be caught dead without a bra. As time has passed, I've become more and more confident in my skin. I rarely think about how different I look because of my headscarf or where I'm from.

Clients just don't give a shit about what I wear or where I'm from as long as I do stellar work and meet deadlines.

The Limiting Belief That Held Me Back for the Longest Time

EVEN AFTER I'D OVERCOME MY INSECURITIES about what I wore and where I was from, there was one limiting belief that I couldn't let go of.

It was believing English was my second language.

Every time I'd sit down to write, it was always in the back of my mind. A freelance writer from Pakistan? What do I know about English? My work's never going to measure up to the work of a native English speaker. But you know what? I learned to speak, read, and write English at the same time as my mother tongue. Which makes English my *first* language.

English is the language I think in.

As much as I'd like to, I can't take the credit for this epiphany. My sister was the one who dropped this truth bomb on me. She and I were talking about how my clients always say, "But your English is so good!" when I tell them I'm from Pakistan. She got the same reaction from almost everyone when she first moved to the United States.

She would simply tell people that while English wasn't her native language, it was her first. And that's why her English was "so" good. My sister now has a PhD and works with a non-profit in Canada. She no longer has to field such questions—but I still do.

So, I now say what she used to: English is my FIRST language. I learned to read, write, and speak it at the same time as my mother tongue, Urdu.

Navigating the Freelance Waters if English is Not Your Native Language

IF YOU'RE A FREELANCER FROM A country where English isn't the native language, there's no need to despair. Learn from my ten-year journey of self-realization and save yourself the insecurities I went through.

Here are a few things you can do:

1. *Take copywriting courses*

   I don't know if it has anything to do with being a non-native English copywriter but I am obsessed with taking online courses. Every time I want to learn a new skill or hone an existing one, I look up a course.

   When I was broke, I looked for free courses. When I could afford them, I went the paid course way. Taking online courses has transformed my writing, business, and life.

   While I enrolled in my first ever paid course (*Damn Fine Words* by James Chartrand), I had one simple goal: become a better writer. But that's not all I became. I also became a confident freelancer and business owner. Taking this course gave me the growth mindset every freelancer needs to succeed.

Wondering what a growth mindset is? It's feeling envious when seeing someone better than us but instead of wallowing in jealousy, your very next questions is, "How do I write like that?" If you've ever stalked a copywriter and wondered how to become as good (or whether you ever will), invest in online courses.

My personal recommendations are *Damn Fine Words* by James Chartrand of Men with Pens, *Guest Blogging Course* by Jon Morrow of Smart Blogger, and *Copy School* by Joanna Wiebe of Copy Hackers.

2. *Learn from other copywriters and freelancers*
If paid courses aren't in the books any time soon, you need to growth hack your learning. Choose three writers/copywriters you wish you could write like. They could be legends or talented copywriters whose work you admire. For me, again, it was James Chartrand of Men with Pens, then Henneke Duistermaat of Enchanting Marketing, and now it's Joanna Wiebe of Copy Hackers.

Once you've made your choice, read everything by these copywriters. Pay attention to how they start a piece, how they transition, even how they format their writing. Look at their conclusions, their call-to-actions, their storytelling tricks.

To get started, the free sixteen-part copywriting course by Henneke Duistermaat of EnchantingMarketing.com will serve you well. You'll receive sixteen emails with easy to implement copywriting tips and learn how to write persuasive content that gets results.

James Chartrand has a free, twenty week writing course on her Damn Fine Words website. It is a masterpiece. Even if you can't afford her flagship writing course, the free course will put you well ahead of the competition.

For books, my personal recommendations are *On Writing* by Stephen King, *Influence* by Robert Caldini, and *The Last Black Unicorn* by Tiffany Haddish. The last one is an unconventional choice but will teach you *so much* if you pay attention to the author's story, her storytelling, and how she deals with everything. It's a must-read book for every struggling freelancer.

3. *Practice what you learn*

You could have access to the most expensive courses, read 100 books a year, or be mentored by Ry Schwartz himself—but it will all be useless if you don't practice what you learn. Whether it's free courses or paid—apply everything you learn. Practice it until it becomes second nature.

Top Tip:
"If there's one thing I've learned from all my mentors, it's to stop calling myself a freelancer. I'm not a freelance writer. I'm an online marketing copywriter and content strategist. I write copy that converts and content that sells. In short, I'm the one businesses go to when they want to make money."

Plenty of copywriters and freelance writers succeed without taking paid courses. You can too if you put in the hours and do the work.

4. *Save praise*

No matter how good you get, it won't count unless you believe it.

Freelancers with English as a second language struggle with this more than others. I know I certainly did. An easy way to counter this is to save *all* the praise you get. Did someone tweet about your article saying how much they loved it? Take a screenshot. A client sends you an email saying this was exactly what they were looking for? Screenshot. Did an influencer say they enjoyed reading your article? You guessed it—screenshot!

Save all the praise you get and put it in a folder on your desktop. Every time you need a confidence boost, go through it.

I wrote about my experience feeling like a fraud in my guest post for Copyblogger too:

I learned this career-saving trick from James Chartrand when I took her *Damn Fine Words* writing course.

One assignment required us to state our limiting beliefs as writers. Guess what mine was? Yep. It was feeling like an impostor.

I felt like I wasn't good enough. I mean, who was I to call myself a writer? English isn't even my first language!

James advised that I collect all the praise I receive and review it whenever I feel like an impostor. And if I don't believe the praise, she suggested that I ask the person who'd given it to me to specify.

I took her advice and now use Evernote to store praise from clients, writers I admire, and random people who sent me a tweet or an email because they appreciated my writing. The collection reminds me of my achievements and always makes me feel better.

**Freelancers with English
as a second language struggle
with this more than others.
I know I certainly did.
An easy way to counter this is
to save ALL the praise you get.
Did someone tweet about your article
saying how much they loved it?
Take a screenshot. A client sends
you an email saying this was
exactly what they were looking for?
Screenshot. Did an influencer say
they enjoyed reading your article?
You guessed it—screenshot!**

Save all the praise you receive, and don't discriminate. Whether it's from someone popular or unknown—praise is praise."

5. *Build your portfolio strategically*
You know how everyone says to blog or guest post to build your portfolio? I recommend the same thing. BUT . . .

You need to be strategic about what you blog about and where you guest post. I mean sure, writing about parenting is great but it won't help you land clients unless that's your target market.

As freelancers our default topic is to write about freelancing and chronicling our journey but please don't. Take it from someone who does have a blog about freelancing. It doesn't help you to land clients because other freelancers following your journey ARE NOT your prospective clients.

In a pinch, yes, you can send whatever writing samples you do have. There are clients who are willing to take a chance on a freelancer if they can demonstrate excellent writing skills.

Whenever possible, blog about topics that are important to your prospective clients. If you're a web writer? Write about writing for the web and connect it to how it can help increase your prospective client's bottom line. Email copywriter? Talk about different email sequences or write about good and bad examples of email newsletters. Want to write blog posts for clients? Talk about how companies can market themselves with a blog and include specific examples.

You are NOT a freelance writer.

IF THERE'S ONE THING I'VE LEARNED from all my mentors, it's to stop calling myself a freelancer.

I'm not a freelance writer. I'm an online marketing copywriter and content strategist. I write copy that converts and content that sells. In short, I'm the one businesses go to when they want to make money.

You are a copywriter. An online marketer. A content strategist. A master of prose. You are whatever type of work you do for your clients without the word "freelance" in front of it.

You are a business owner. You are always a partner, never an employee. You are the boss.

© Photo by Judd Weiss

ABOUT THE EDITOR

ERIN WILDERMUTH IS AN ECONOMIC PHILOSOPHER, writer, photographer, and travel vagabond with a Master's Degree in International Political Economy from the London School of Economics. Her Master's thesis concentrated on how the digital divide impacts global decision making and international labor markets. She has been intent upon shedding light on how global trends and technological advances can help people rise from economic exploitation into economic independence ever since. Her work has appeared in such diverse publications as the *Huffington Post, American Spectator,* and *Scuba Diver Magazine.*

Erin left the 9-to-5 herself, negotiating a part-time, remote arrangement with her employer. Within a year, she was working full-time as a freelance underwater photographer, videographer and writer in Thailand. She lived in Asia for two years and has since returned to the United States, using her freelance income to return to school where she is studying regenerative medicine. She currently lives in Baltimore, MD.

Recent and Forthcoming Books from Three Rooms Press

FICTION

Meagan Brothers
Weird Girl and What's His Name

Ron Dakron
Hello Devilfish!

Michael T. Fournier
Hidden Wheel
Swing State

William Least Heat-Moon
Celestial Mechanics

Aimee Herman
Everything Grows

Eamon Loingsigh
Light of the Diddicoy
Exile on Bridge Street

John Marshall
The Greenfather

Aram Saroyan
Still Night in L.A.

Richard Vetere
The Writers Afterlife
Champagne and Cocaine

Julia Watts
Quiver

MEMOIR & BIOGRAPHY

**Nassrine Azimi and
Michel Wasserman**
*Last Boat to Yokohama:
The Life and Legacy of
Beate Sirota Gordon*

William S. Burroughs & Allen Ginsberg
*Don't Hide the Madness:
William S. Burroughs in Conversation
with Allen Ginsberg*
edited by Steven Taylor

James Carr
*BAD: The Autobiography of
James Carr*

Richard Katrovas
*Raising Girls in Bohemia:
Meditations of an American Father; A
Memoir in Essays*

Judith Malina
*Full Moon Stages:
Personal Notes from
50 Years of The Living Theatre*

Phil Marcade
*Punk Avenue:
Inside the New York City
Underground, 1972-1982*

Alvin Orloff
*Disasterama! Adventures in the Queer
Underground 1977–1997*

Stephen Spotte
*My Watery Self:
Memoirs of a Marine Scientist*

PHOTOGRAPHY-MEMOIR

Mike Watt
On & Off Bass

SHORT STORY ANTHOLOGIES

SINGLE AUTHOR

The Alien Archives: Stories
by Robert Silverberg

First-Person Singularities: Stories
by Robert Silverberg
with an introduction by John Scalzi

Tales from the Eternal Café: Stories
by Janet Hamill, with an introduction
by Patti Smith

*Time and Time Again:
Sixteen Trips in Time*
by Robert Silverberg

MULTI-AUTHOR

*Crime + Music: Twenty Stories
of Music-Themed Noir*
edited by Jim Fusilli

Dark City Lights: New York Stories
edited by Lawrence Block

*Florida Happens:
Bouchercon 2018 Anthology*
edited by Greg Herren

*Have a NYC I, II & III:
New York Short Stories;*
edited by Peter Carlaftes
& Kat Georges

*Songs of My Selfie:
An Anthology of Millennial Stories*
edited by Constance Renfrow

*The Obama Inheritance:
15 Stories of Conspiracy Noir*
edited by Gary Phillips

*This Way to the End Times:
Classic and New Stories of
the Apocalypse*
edited by Robert Silverberg

MIXED MEDIA

John S. Paul
Sign Language: A Painter's Notebook
(photography, poetry and prose)

FILM & PLAYS

Israel Horovitz
*My Old Lady: Complete Stage Play
and Screenplay with an Essay on
Adaptation*

Peter Carlaftes
Triumph For Rent (3 Plays)
Teatrophy (3 More Plays)

Kat Georges
*Three Somebodies: Plays about
Notorious Dissidents*

HUMOR

Peter Carlaftes
A Year on Facebook

DADA

*Maintenant: A Journal of
Contemporary Dada Writing & Art
(Annual, since 2008)*

TRANSLATIONS

Thomas Bernhard
On Earth and in Hell
(poems of Thomas Bernhard
with English translations by
Peter Waugh)

Patrizia Gattaceca
Isula d'Anima / Soul Island
(poems by the author
in Corsican with English
translations)

César Vallejo | Gerard Malanga
Malanga Chasing Vallejo
(selected poems of César Vallejo
with English translations
and additional notes by
Gerard Malanga)

George Wallace
EOS: Abductor of Men
(selected poems in Greek & English)

ESSAY COLLECTION

*Womentality: Thirteen Empowering Stories
by Everyday Women Who Said Goodbye to
the Workplace and Hello to Their Lives*
edited by Erin Wildermuth

POETRY COLLECTIONS

Hala Alyan
Atrium

Peter Carlaftes
DrunkYard Dog
I Fold with the Hand I Was Dealt

Thomas Fucaloro
It Starts from the Belly and Blooms
*Inheriting Craziness is Like
a Soft Halo of Light*

Kat Georges
Our Lady of the Hunger

Robert Gibbons
Close to the Tree

Israel Horovitz
Heaven and Other Poems

David Lawton
Sharp Blue Stream

Jane LeCroy
Signature Play

Philip Meersman
This is Belgian Chocolate

Jane Ormerod
Recreational Vehicles on Fire
Welcome to the Museum of Cattle

Lisa Panepinto
On This Borrowed Bike

George Wallace
Poppin' Johnny

Three Rooms Press | New York, NY | Current Catalog: www.threeroomspress.com
Three Rooms Press books are distributed by PGW/Ingram: www.pgw.com